Praise for the second edition:

"I profoundly reject the idea that th[...]
doing business responsibly and goo[...]
is true. Indeed, Andy's book sho[...]
unlocks superior performance. As such, it's a must-read for any brand or business."

— *Alan Jope, CEO, Unilever*

"The purpose of a corporation has never been more important than it is today. And Andy's latest update to *Business on a Mission* does a terrific job of explaining both how and why this is so. Combining case studies and proven models with personal anecdotes, the book is a must-read for anyone interested in the larger purpose of business in society – highly recommend!"

— *Michael Roth, Executive Chairman,*
Interpublic Group (IPG)

Praise for the first edition:

"This book is a timely reminder that the primary purpose of business has always been to serve a clear social need. The message is brilliantly combined with a well-illustrated roadmap of how we can get back to that essential objective."

— *Paul Polman, CEO, Unilever 2009–2019*

"In *Business on a Mission*, Andy Last describes how business can develop to deliver to a purpose that serves society. Companies who are able to do this are magnets for employees who we recognise as increasingly concerned to find meaning in their work. He describes, too, how NGOs and business can work together for good, with clarity about motive being vital for partnerships to work. Together, business and NGOs can make a bigger difference in the world than either can achieve alone."

— *Dame Barbara Stocking, President, Murray Edwards College,*
University of Cambridge, and former CEO, Oxfam

engaging and a must-read for anyone interested in making business better."

— *Marc Van Ameringen, Executive Director, Global Alliance for Improved Nutrition (GAIN) 2005–2016*

"From 2005 to 2011, I had the privilege to drive one of the biggest transformations in corporate strategy to integrate social, economic and environmental insights into the innovation agenda of all categories and brands at Unilever. We called this innovation model the 'Brand Imprint.' We knew that the care we put into the community and environment is intrinsically connected with the power of those brands to engage people not only as consumers, but also as citizens and brand advocates. Andy and Richard, founders of salt, were key partners in that process. This book will help many other businesses leverage the power of brands to create a better future. We all need to find new, more sustainable ways of living, and brand innovation will play a pivotal role in that agenda."

— *Santiago Gowland, CEO, Rainforest Alliance*

"Andy Last is a seasoned professional in the sustainability space and his book, *Business on a Mission*, cuts through the purpose fluff and offers practical advice for any company that wants to walk the talk."

— *Thomas Kolster, Mr Goodvertising, author and sustainability thought-leader*

BUSINESS ON A MISSION

Business on a Mission is a simple to follow guide for how organisations can adapt to the changing world and evolving expectations of stakeholders to build more purpose-led, sustainable businesses. It features proven models and case study examples of how to create a brand that talks to the emerging Gen Z consumer base; how to use social missions to drive sales in retail and with B2B customers; how to preserve reputation and licence to operate by working in partnership with not-for-profit organisations; and how to attract and retain the best talent by demonstrating a genuine social purpose.

As well as clear, applicable models and behind-the-scenes descriptions of how successful campaigns were built and sustainable change made, this book features candid interviews with change makers from the worlds of retail, professional services, consumer goods, and NGOs. This second edition looks at how businesses and brands like Dove are now linking social and environmental goals, with an exclusive interview with Unilever CEO, Alan Jope. It explores how investors are now driving a systemic change in focus in the boardroom towards the sustainability agenda, and how leaders can respond to this, featuring a new interview with Frank Cooper, Global Chief Marketing Officer and member of the Global Executive Committee at BlackRock. The impact of the pandemic on what it means to be a sustainable brand, including a focus on sustainable supply chains, the growing power of Gen Z, the growth of online purchasing, multi-stakeholder partnerships, increased regulation, and culture at work, is also explored.

This book has been read, enjoyed, and used by business leaders to identify models for change; by managers to create progressive campaigns; by NGOs to create stronger partnerships with the private sector; and by students to learn how theories of social purpose and sustainability can be applied in the real world. The first edition was Bronze winner of the AXIOM Business Book Award in the category of *Philanthropy, Non-Profit, Sustainability*.

Andy Last co-founded salt in 2000 and led the development of the company's Social Mission approach to create sustainable, progressive campaigns for brands and businesses. He has worked since 2006 on Lifebuoy soap's award-winning social mission, described as the "best social program ever" by David Aaker, Professor Emeritus at the Haas School of Business. He led salt to be in the first group of UK companies to be accredited as a B-Corporation in 2015 and is now a B-Corp Ambassador as well as a member of the Medinge Group, the brands with a conscience think tank.

BUSINESS ON A MISSION

HOW TO BUILD A SUSTAINABLE BRAND

Second Edition

Andy Last

Routledge
Taylor & Francis Group

LONDON AND NEW YORK

Cover image: © Andy Last

Second edition published 2022
by Routledge
4 Park Square, Milton Park, Abingdon, Oxon, OX14 4RN

and by Routledge
605 Third Avenue, New York, NY 10158

Routledge is an imprint of the Taylor & Francis Group, an informa business

© 2022 Andy Last

First edition published by Routledge 2016

British Library Cataloguing-in-Publication Data
A catalogue record for this book is available from the British Library

Library of Congress Cataloging-in-Publication Data
A catalog record has been requested for this book

ISBN: 978-1-032-01024-3 (hbk)
ISBN: 978-1-032-00941-4 (pbk)
ISBN: 978-1-003-17681-7 (ebk)

DOI: 10.4324/9781003176817

Typeset in Bembo
by codeMantra

CONTENTS

CONTENTS

ACKNOWLEDGEMENTS

This book is the result of the programmes I have been privileged enough to work on and the people I've been lucky enough to work with. My first trip to Kibera changed my life because of the work I saw there and the people I met, in particular Myriam Sidibe and Val Curtis. This part of the story is told in this book, but it can't do justice to the inspiration they have been to me and countless others.

Val Curtis did so much to pioneer the cause of better public health through improved hygiene and sanitation. She kept inspiring us all throughout her final illness in 2020, not least in her work to tackle the Covid-19 pandemic. Val gave her inaugural lecture for the London School of Hygiene and Tropical Medicine just weeks before she died and gave it with typical clarity, extraordinary courage, and a beautifully blunt call to action to all of her audience to continue her work. This second edition is, I hope, a small contribution to that effort.

I will be forever grateful to the hundreds of friends and colleagues at salt who have been part of this movement over the years, but especially to Marianne Blamire (because Global Handwashing Day will always be on October 15th not the 16th), to Taryn Malakou, who has persuaded more brands than any of us could have imagined that they really can do well by doing good, and to Richard Cox and Nicky Young for building our business on a mission together. I am also hugely thankful to our new friends at MullenLowe who have been so supportive of our work.

I owe a huge debt to the Lifebuoy team for allowing me to feel such a part of it over the last 15 years (Steve Miles, Shweta Harit, Samir Singh, Anila Gopal, Anusha Gupta, Kartik Chandrasekhar, and countless other dedicated and fun crusaders); to the sustainability champions at Unilever, who have given more inspiration to more people than they realise; and to the wise people in all the other businesses who have been kind enough to trust us.

I am equally in debt to the dedicated people in the NGOs, charities, and social enterprises who have been generous with their advice and insights and who have always brought me back to what matters.

I am very grateful to the people who gave their valuable time to be interviewed for this book: Marc van Ameringen, Adam Elman, Alan Jope, Mike Mack, Paul Polman, Jonas Prising, Madhu Rao, Myriam Sidibe, and Matt Stone.

I have been lucky enough in life to have had two sons as well as two brothers to stop me getting above myself, to forgive my mistakes, and to be there when it really counts. Henry, Jordan, Philip, and Peter – thank you for being my first and last friends.

And finally to my mum, Sue, who continues to dedicate her life to helping others. Hopefully a thank you in print makes up a little bit for all the times I forgot in real life.

INTRODUCTION TO THE
SECOND EDITION

Since the publication of the first edition in December 2016 there have been three major developments that have affected the role of business in society:

1   Expectations on business in relation to the environment have shifted from avoiding doing harm to actively developing solutions. The "War on Plastic" – triggered by David Attenborough's Blue Planet II series in 2017 – created a groundswell of mass public concern and political pressure for action that goes well beyond the previous campaigning of "dark green" environmentalists. And businesses everywhere – as well as governments – have had to pay attention to the organised voices of Extinction Rebellion and other campaigners. Businesses and brands can no longer promote social initiatives or claim to be "purpose-led" if they are not actively tackling their own and their whole value chains' environmental outputs, from carbon emissions to plastic wrappers.

2   Investors are now turning to companies with solid ESG (environmental, social, and governance) credentials. Again, this reflects a change from this being the concern of specialist impact investors, to it becoming a driver of mainstream investment decisions. The growing belief among investors and analysts that positive ESG credentials make for better returns on their investments has led them to question how well traditional financial models can assess the risks and opportunities associated with ESG performance adequately. If Blue Planet II was the bellwether of the move of environmentalism from a pressing concern of the few

to a daily reality for the many, so Larry Fink, the chief executive of BlackRock, the world's largest asset manager with some $6.5 trillion in assets under management, has been for the investment world. In his 2018 annual letter to the companies his firm invests in, he wrote, "Without a sense of purpose, no company, either public or private, can achieve its full potential." Whether passive or active, investors are encouraging companies to improve their social and environmental performance. Why? Because they have watched, researched, analysed, and interrogated companies' performance (more than any protestor, regulator, or activist citizen was ever able to do) and come to the conclusion that companies who are not acting on their material environmental and social impacts are not worth investing in.

This change in the focus of even the most hard-nosed investors is perhaps the single-most reassuring signal for those who fear businesses' engagement in societal and environmental issues amount to little more than purposewash and greenwash and this second edition includes a new chapter, "How sustainable brands are winning on Wall Street."

3   The third change is the most recent, the impact of the Covid-19 pandemic on the relationship between business and society, and how it has forced companies in all sectors to demonstrate what they actually do to contribute to society. This can be seen as an acceleration of what was already happening, but what Covid-19 and our response to it as individuals and communities, businesses, and nations has shown is that none of us – and certainly no business – can function independently from society. Society exists and companies now, more than ever, need to be able to demonstrate how they contribute to it across every aspect of their business. This edition looks at the impact of the pandemic on what it means to be a sustainable brand, including the growing power of Gen Z, the growth of online purchasing, and the changing nature of culture at work.

I hope this new edition succeeds in its ambition of helping more businesses take more positive steps towards being more sustainable – environmentally, socially, and commercially.

FROM WEST KIRBY TO KIBERA ...
AND BACK AGAIN

For most people in the world, 2020 was a year like no other. As the pandemic challenged governments to respond to a public health crisis and its repercussions across all elements of life, it accelerated the demands for action on climate change and social justice. It was also the year that this story and Lifebuoy soap came back to the UK, full circle from Kibera to West Kirby, as handwashing with soap became a topic of global importance.

★★★

I grew up close to Port Sunlight on the Wirral, across the River Mersey from Liverpool. We lived in West Kirby, not far from the port that William Hesketh Lever had built in the late 19th century to take advantage of the trade routes in and out of Liverpool, then the busiest port in the world. Lever was the founder of Lever Brothers, later to become Unilever, and one of those public-minded industrialists of Victorian England whose approach to business was openly driven by a desire to make things better.

As children, we used to get taken to the Lady Lever Art Gallery on rainy Sundays, and to the village Lever had built to house his workforce. We got to know the stories of this man – how he built beautiful homes for his workers so that they might lead "more fulfilling, productive lives." About the global business empire he built from the Wirral in the 19th century by "making cleanliness commonplace." And how he created Lifebuoy, an affordable bar of soap that the poor in Liverpool could use literally to save their lives by handwashing with soap to protect themselves from cholera and other

DOI: 10.4324/9781003176817-1

infectious diseases that were sweeping through the overcrowded slums of a rapidly expanding city. Selling soap then – as now – had a purpose.

Even as children it was easy to see the link between Lever doing good for society and doing well for his business. He built his workers decent homes so that he could have a more productive workforce. He created an affordable way for people to protect themselves from disease so that he could sell more soap. There was a plain-speaking logic that often seems to get lost today when business leaders talk about purpose and present "doing good" initiatives as driven by higher motives than merely making money.

Lever was open about his motives. There was no embarrassment, no pretence, no hiding what the business was about. He didn't park "doing good" in philanthropy or corporate social responsibility. His purpose and business motives were one and the same: his business mission was a social one.

Fast-forward 30 years from those trips to Port Sunlight to 2006. I was asked by Unilever to visit a handwashing project being run in Kibera, in Nairobi, Kenya. There, the company was using that same soap, Lifebuoy, to tackle those same diseases in similarly over-crowded slums. I'd been sent because this sounded like a "good PR story." But I met some incredible people in Kibera, who helped change everything: in particular, Myriam Sidibe, who had recently joined Unilever from the development sector, and who is inter-viewed in this book, and Val Curtis, director of the Hygiene Centre at the London School of Hygiene and Tropical Medicine, and a world expert in hygiene and behaviour change.[1]

In Kibera I saw handwashing lessons in schools – Lifebuoy teach-ing children and parents how they could protect themselves from diseases. Each year over two million children fail to reach their fifth birthday because of diarrhoeal diseases and pneumonia.[2] The simple act of handwashing with soap at the appropriate time could cut this number in half, as William Lever knew. But Lever might also have pointed out that the story here was not one of Lifebuoy's philan-thropy nor Unilever's corporate social responsibility, it was how the company was building its business in Africa by giving it a social mission. More people washing their hands more often meant more lives saved and more soap sold. The real Lifebuoy story was what it had always been: growing a business through a social mission.

When we got back to London, we set up an interview with the *Financial Times*, and the resulting story, "Unilever looks to clean up in Africa," couldn't have been clearer about the link between business and society and the business case for having a social mission.[3]

That straight-talking position was born in Port Sunlight and set the tone for how Lifebuoy went about its social mission to bring health and hygiene to a billion people. It has helped build more open, trusting partnerships with non-governmental organisations (NGOs), academics, governments, and charities; helped engage consumers in-store and on social media networks; helped put Unilever alongside Google and Apple as one of the most sought-after employers in the world[4]; and helped the Lifebuoy business more than double in value in the five years from 2008.

In doing so, Lifebuoy has helped over a billion people develop better handwashing habits and been described as having the "best social program ever" by David Aaker, professor emeritus at the Haas School of Business.[5]

This book tells not just the Lifebuoy story but the wider story of how business lost and then refound its social purpose and how different organisations have developed social missions. It includes interviews conducted specially for this book with leading figures who have transformed the way their companies do business, case studies illustrating how those companies and others have developed more sustainable brands, and research into the attitudes of the post-millennial Generation Z that will shape how business and society interact in the coming decades.

It offers practical guidance for those who want to build sustainable brands, with clear criteria for what makes a good social mission, a step-by-step process for building one, and guidelines for developing partnerships and communications strategies.

•••

Not all businesses demonstrate their connection to society as obviously as William Lever did with his model village and brand names like Lifebuoy that called out the good they promised to do. But all businesses at their core do have to serve society. Businesses ultimately have to sell products or services to people, and people are society. Businesses have always had to have a social mission in that sense.

In a simple community, the connection between business and society is simple to see. The business can only find customers if it is providing something of value to that community. Investors will only lend capital to the business owner if they can see the future value of the business and what it does. And any harm caused by that business is quickly self-regulated by customers, suppliers, employees, and investors who know each other and can see all impacts clearly enough.

This belief, this close connection between business and society, drove the "Enlightened Entrepreneurs" (also the title of Ian Bradley's book about Victorian business leaders like William Lever, George Cadbury, Joseph Rowntree, and Jesse Boot) to build enduring businesses that insisted this connection between business and society could not be broken.[6] Their values and their businesses lasted so long in no small part because their founders and founding principles forced them never to forget that business and society were inextricably linked.

Today, these companies still talk about their principles in terms that link the way they do business to their wider role in society. Unilever's stated vision, for example, is to "decouple growth from our environmental impact, while increasing our positive social impact" – an impact that was defined as helping a billion people improve their health and well-being by 2020, an appropriately sized target for a company whose products are used by more than two billion people a day, and a target still underpinned by handwashing with soap.[7]

Companies like these helped drive growth in 19th-century Great Britain after the first industrial revolution, and the same philosophical approach helped create some of the most successful and enduring businesses in other parts of Europe. J.C. Jacobsen founded Carlsberg in 1847 and felt a clear social obligation to his workers, providing them with medical aid, pension schemes, and funeral assistance, at a time when the state provided no social safety net.

Across the Atlantic, the second industrial revolution was built on the Puritan principles that had crossed on the Mayflower. The "moral outlook that subordinated the interests of the individual to the group," the Puritan belief that drove the pilgrims in their journey towards the New World, laid the origins of American managerial culture, as described in *The Puritan Gift*, by Kenneth Hopper

and William Hopper.[8] These were translated into th
of Management in the US through the first half of the
and when General MacArthur took these principles t
oversaw the occupation in the aftermath of the Secon
they helped create the ingredients for the third indu
tion, the electronics boom driven from Japan in the s
the 20th century.

These three great leaps forward were each propelled by a clear
connection between business and society. They happened because
the owners and managers of businesses not only recognised the
inherent connection between business and society but also geared
their enterprises to progress in a way that benefited from that connection. They knew that their growth would be bigger and more
enduring if they interwove it with society.

This is not corporate social responsibility. It is simply a recogni-
tion that businesses grow better and more sustainably when they are
aligned to the goals of society. It is social opportunity, rather than
responsibility.

Adam Smith's most famous quote, from *The Wealth of Nations* –
"It is not from the benevolence of the butcher, the brewer, or
the baker that we expect our dinner, but from their regard to
their own interest"[9] – has often been taken as a killer point from
the father of modern economics in the case against business
engaging with society. Business has to be selfish, the argument
goes, and this means focussing on commercial rather than societal
benefits.

But Smith was also clear that human nature is not just selfish but,
in fact, has a sympathy for the situation of others. The opening line
of his first book, *The Theory of Moral Sentiments* (a book he himself
thought the better of the two works, and to which here turned
shortly before his death with ongoing refinements and adjustments)
reads: "How selfish soever man may be supposed, there are evidently
some principles in his nature, which interest him in the fortune of
others, and render their happiness necessary to him, though he
derives nothing from it except the pleasure of seeing it."[10] And he
saw that inequality wasn't sustainable: "No society can surely be
flourishing and happy, of which the far greater part of the members
are poor and miserable." For Smith, the "commercial society" placed
business firmly in the context of society.

ıuman beings are social animals with selfish genes and we flour-
ın when the two work in tandem. Likewise for businesses –
successful, sustainable growth is most easily achieved when a
business's selfish, competitive instincts are harnessed to the needs of
the society in which it operates.

People like William Lever never talked about doing good or
giving back to society. He was a businessman. He wouldn't have
disagreed with Milton Friedman's argument that managers have one
responsibility and one responsibility only: namely, to do the bidding
of their employers, and ultimately the owners of the business.[11] That
there is no such thing as a separate corporate social responsibility.

But Lever and others like him recognised that the sustained success of their businesses depended on the social context. That their
businesses existed only in that context, and that the more opportunities
they could harness for society the more successful their businesses
would be.

They focussed not on the positive impact business could have on
society, but on the positive impact society could have on business.
Getting business leaders – who become leaders by being expert at
managing business not society – to look at things this way round
opens up far greater opportunities for progress for all. In fact, many
of today's most iconic companies began with the stated intention of
helping those in need. John Harvey Kellogg developed corn flakes
initially to offer a more nutritious breakfast to the American poor.
Isaac Carasso – founder of Danone – began making and selling
yoghurt when he saw children in his home country of Spain suffer-
ing from intestinal problems at the end of the First World War.
They created businesses based on meeting a clear social need of their
time.

Lifebuoy proved its lasting social value by returning to the UK in
2020 in response to the clear social need of this time – to enable
people to protect themselves through the enduring power of
handwashing with soap. And that a clear, social purpose is central to
building a sustainable brand.

So, if the relationship between business and society is so potent,
why did we forget it? Why did business move away from its close
connection to society, and why did society become so suspicious of
business and its motives?

NOTES

1 Val pioneered much of today's thinking around human behaviour and hygiene, and new ways to improve public health, and in 2020 was invited to contribute to the SAGE committee to advise on the UK's response to COVID-19. Val died in October 2020 but not before campaigning fiercely against the impact of government austerity on the National Health Service (https://www.theguardian.com/commentisfree/2020/jul/16/extra-cancer-deaths-this-year-covid19-nhs-health) and giving the people she left behind our "marching orders" to continue her work.

2 UNICEF (2012). Pneumonia and diarrhoea: Tackling the deadliest diseases for the world's poorest children. http://www.unicef.org/eapro/Pneumonia_and_Diarrhoea_Report_2012.pdf.

3 Jopson, B. (2007, 15 November). Unilever looks to clean up in Africa. *Financial Times*. http://www.ft.com/cms/s/0/47b3586c-931f-11dc-ad39-0000779fd2ac.html.

4 Wartzman, R. (2015, 7 January). What Unilever shares with Google and Apple. *Fortune*. http://fortune.com/2015/01/07/what-unilever-shares-with-google-and-apple.

5 Aaker, D. (2015, 19 October). Lifebuoy: The best social responsibility program ever? https://www.linkedin.com/pulse/lifebuoy-best-social-program-ever-davidaaker.

6 Bradley, I.C. (2007). *Enlightened Entrepreneurs: Business Ethics in Victorian Britain*. Oxford: Lion.

7 Unilever (n.d.). Our strategy for sustainable business. https://www.unilever.com/sustainable-living/the-sustainable-living-plan/our-strategy.

8 Hopper, K. and Hopper W. (2009). *The Puritan Gift*. London: I.B. Tauris.

9 Smith, A. (1776). *An Inquiry into the Nature and Causes of the Wealth of Nations*. London: Dent, 1957, 2 vols.: Chapter 2.

10 Smith, A. (1759). *The Theory of Moral Sentiments*. Oxford: Clarendon, 1976: Part I, Section I, Chapter I.

11 Friedman, M. (1970, 13 September). The social responsibility of business to increase its profits. *New York Times Magazine*. http://www.colorado.edu/studentgroups/libertarians/issues/friedman-soc-respbusiness.html.

2

DIVERGING AGENDAS AND THE AGE OF TRANSPARENCY

Two primary factors caused business and society to diverge in the second half of the 20th century: a change in the way business success was defined and rewarded, and a change in our notion of society and therefore the social context in which business is expected to operate.

The first factor began when the performance of business leaders – the people in corporations charged with delivering a return on capital to owners and investors – started being judged not by people who knew the day-to-day realities of those businesses, but by invisible shareholders through faraway and increasingly opaque financial markets.

Others have spoken far more powerfully on this. David Simon, creator of *The Wire*, for example, said,

> That may be the ultimate tragedy of capitalism in our time, that it has achieved its dominance without regard to a social compact, without being connected to any other metric for human progress. We understand profit. In my country we measure things by profit. We listen to the Wall Street analysts. They tell us what we're supposed to do every quarter. The quarterly report is God. Turn to face God. Turn to face Mecca, you know. Did you make your number? Did you not make your number? Do you want your bonus? Do you not want your bonus? And that notion that capital is the metric, that profit is the metric by which we're going to measure the health of our society is one of the fundamental mistakes of the last 30 years. I would date it in my country to about 1980 exactly, and it has triumphed.[1]

DOI: 10.4324/9781003176817-2

When the relationship moves from personal to institutional, and access to capital moves from known investors to the "faceless banks" of *The Grapes of Wrath* – the "creatures" that "breathe profits" and "eat the interest on money" – the connection between business and society can stretch too thin.[2] Today's rarefied capital markets and complex investment vehicles have almost inevitably led to the sort of "institutional amorality" we have seen in the financial sector, where investors can't see the connection between business and society, and business leaders are therefore judged by metrics that discount that connection.

The 2008 financial collapse can be seen as the beginning of the end of this disconnect, and we may look back on it as having marked the start of a new, sustainable growth model based on a renewed alignment between the business and society. Some business leaders have reasserted the connection explicitly. Speaking in Paris at the time, Frank Riboud, then chairman of Groupe Danone, said,

> A company only exists and lasts because it creates value for the whole of society [...] a company's raison d'être is its social usefulness. That means serving society – men and women – in their everyday lives, through products, services, work or the dividends it pays.[3]

More recently, the American Business Roundtable – an organisation that represents the CEOs of America's leading companies – updated its Statement on the Purpose of a Corporation to "move away from shareholder primacy" to "include a commitment to all stakeholders." Their new definition recognised the need for business to pay regard to the interests of all stakeholders – customers, employees, suppliers, and communities, not just shareholders. In other words, a return to the old understanding that business needed to recognise and act on its connection to society. Michael Roth, executive chairman of Interpublic Group (IPG), was a signatory to that statement and is interviewed in Chapter 7 of this book.

The second factor has been the broadening definition of what society means for many businesses: that their "community" is no longer confined to the immediate surroundings of their factories and offices. In a globalised economy, the connections between business and society, so visible locally, can become invisible and unguarded.

So the inequitable treatment of workers in the supply chain in far-off lands, or the unsustainable sourcing of commodities from forests and mines in other part of the world, could become commonplace, facilitated by cheaper and quicker global transportation but invisible to customers in the marketplace. In a closer, more local society, such practices would be more easily visible and less easily tolerated. Faraway, they could be ignored.

But now, the transparency of the digital age shines a light into every dark corner of business, every shadowy place where the connection with society may have been forgotten.

Treating workers like slaves is becoming toxic for businesses; ignoring the social impacts of supply chains threatens their reputations and ability to do business. Nike, for example, originally responded to accusations of using sweatshop labour in the 1990s by denying any malpractice in its supplier factories and arguing that they didn't control what went on in those factories anyway, because they weren't part of Nike. That changed as digital communications not only made the invisible visible, but enabled campaigners to mobilise people to action, or in the case of buying Nike trainers, inaction, through consumer "buycotts."

Today, Nike's sense of accountability for what goes on in its supply chain is radically different. It states that "[o]ne of our responsibilities as a global company is to play a role in bringing about positive, systemic change for workers within our supply chain and in the industry."[4] It publishes the names and addresses of all contract factories that make its products and has signed up to the Fair Labor Association, allowing them to conduct unannounced audits of all Nike's supplier sites.

Modern communications are reasserting the primacy of the connection between business and society and extending the scope of the communities and society for which a business is expected to take responsibility. The commercial risk of forgetting the social connection is overtaking the cost benefits of taking those shortcuts. Businesses now need to manage their connection with society carefully to avoid customer boycotts, social media outings, and regulators limiting their licence to operate.

In 2020, this expectation on businesses reached the point where businesses were expected not only to manage their own direct and indirect impacts on society, but also to express their point of view about society in general. In the protests following the killing of George Floyd by police in Minneapolis, companies came under pressure not to do nothing. "To be silent is to be complicit. Black Lives Matter," tweeted Netflix. Businesses are part of society whether they want to be or not, and they are being observed and judged by how they manage that connection.

In this interconnected world, our definition of society is growing to encompass not only our neighbours and compatriots but people from all corners of the world with whom we can connect in an instant. The societal context in which businesses operate now encompasses this broader community, with customers in one part of the world holding businesses to account for how raw materials are sourced by people on the opposite side of the planet, coupled with a growing understanding of the limits of the planet's resources.

These planetary constraints and questions around a more equitable way of doing business in a globalised, increasingly transparent world form the new social context in which business operates. Business leaders today must ask themselves the same question that successful businesses of previous generations asked themselves: how do we lead our business to lasting success in this social context?

The businesses that did this in the past are the ones whose names endure today. The businesses that do it today will be the ones that build sustainable brands for tomorrow.

•••

Is the understanding of this new, global social context starting to drive a fourth industrial revolution? One in which sustainable brands and sustainable development challenge the neoliberal consensus that private enterprise should be freed from the shackles of the state? Certainly, many business leaders are realigning themselves and their businesses to acknowledge their "social compact."

At the forefront have been those companies whose business depends most on public goodwill, those with relatively low-cost goods that are dependent on brand image and frequent purchase and therefore susceptible to instant losses should the goodwill of their brands be diminished – companies like Nestlé, Nike, and Coca-Cola.

Nestlé: Former President of Corporate Affairs Paul Bakus, in 2014

More or less all business started out with a social purpose of some kind, so the future may look more like a rediscovery of the social purpose of business. What's been lost in recent decades is the long term perspective, values-based behaviors grounded in respect, and interconnectivity between the needs of society and the innovative dynamism of business.[5]

Nike: Former CEO Mark Parker, in 2010

It took us a while, but we finally figured out that we could apply these two core competencies – design and innovation – to bring about environmental, labor and social change. We opened the aperture of our lens and discovered our potential to have a positive influence on waste reduction, climate change, managing natural resources, renewable energy and factory conditions. We saw that doing the right thing was good for business today – and would be an engine for our growth in the near future.[6]

Coca-Cola: Former Chairman and CEO, Muhtar Kent, in 2013

There's been a significant shift in consumer attitudes towards large, global enterprises, particularly those with brands that are an everyday part of their lives. It used to be, a generation ago, that businesses were expected to create value for a narrower group of stakeholders, including customers, business partners and shareowners. Today, we need to create value for a broader range of people and organisations, from governments and non-governmental organisations to environmental and health-related partners. As we strive to make a positive difference in the world, we now work with 'golden triangle' partners across business, government and civil society.[7]

Most prominent in this restatement of the relationship between business and society has been Paul Polman, CEO of Unilever from 2009 to 2019. Soon after his appointment, he announced that the company would no longer provide quarterly profit updates to investors, saying,

Unilever has been around for 100–plus years. We want to be around for several hundred more. If you buy into this long-term value-creation model, which is equitable, which is shared, which is sustainable, then come and invest with us. If you don't buy into this, I respect you as a human being, but don't put your money in our company.[8]

He saw short-termism in the financial community as a barrier to the company's growth because it was incompatible with an approach that linked business and society. Like William Lever some 130 years previously, he was tying the success of the business to its social context.

Among his other positions, Polman is on the Board of the Global Compact (a United Nations pact to encourage businesses to adopt sustainable and socially responsible policies) and served on the High Level Panel of Eminent Persons looking at the Post-2015 Development Agenda for former UN secretary-general, Ban-Ki Moon (what eventually became the Sustainable Development Goals), giving him a unique perspective on the connection between business and society. This interview, as well as those in the following chapters, was given exclusively for this book, and took place while he was still CEO of Unilever.

Paul Polman

I have always believed that the purpose of business is to serve, not take from, society. It needs to address some of the challenges out there positively to gain its legitimacy. Not being less bad or CSR, but truly making a positive contribution. Shareholder primacy has become the driving force for many. If we put serving society squarely back in the middle, we will create better longer-term sustainable business models and the shareholder will ultimately be rewarded as well.

When I came to Unilever, the company wasn't doing particularly well and the model needed to be changed in many ways. However, as Jim Collins says in *Good to Great*,[9] you need to nurture the core before you stimulate progress. That core for Unilever was a strong social consciousness, but it was not always linked to driving the business. Doing good to some extent was decoupled from doing well. A little bit like overseas development aid.

Then the crisis of 2008 happened, just when I came in, which made a lot of us reflect on what we were doing as a society as a whole. What you see in the previous 10–15-year period is all these forces coming together that the world has not faced before. Rapid economic growth with resulting pressure on planetary boundaries such as climate change; the changing political balance and lack of global governance; increasingly uneven income distribution. People started to realise that wealth was going to too few people and not distributed, which wasn't good enough.

The crisis of 2007/2008, which I have often called a moral crisis, made us realise that a system of enormous public and private debt, overconsumption and frankly leaving too many behind was simply not sustainable. While wealth might be concentrated, consumers increasingly have power because of the web and that has created new dynamics and demands on companies and governments alike.

So you have to work harder to be part of the solution and business leaders need to understand that. People have the power of the wallet and they will increasingly only support companies that are responsible and that make a positive contribution. Manipulating Libor or foreign exchange rates, selling horse meat instead of beef, buying textiles from a collapsing factory or cheating on emission standards is just not cool anymore. In this age of transparency, the market capitalisation of companies (for which read 'reputation') can change fast.

What we are really now asking is: how can you create a business model that goes beyond shared value to a net positive impact? Actively helping solve issues that we face such as increasing youth unemployment; 800 million people still going to bed hungry; 2.5 billon without adequate sanitation; 750 million with no access to clean drinking water; 170 million children stunted every year. And the list goes on. What are you doing to make a positive contribution, or are you just here to make things worse? What are you doing to bring clean drinking water to these people? What are you doing to reduce issues of child mortality?

That fits our business model very well but, frankly it should fit any business model because business should be there to serve, not take from, society.

When we came up with the Unilever Sustainable Living Plan (USLP), a lot of people were sceptical, a lot of people were hesitant, a lot of people were nervous, like with any major change effort.

It is, indeed, a very audacious vision with very ambitious targets that even made us nervous; although if you are not nervous you probably have not pushed the boundaries far enough. But when we launched the USLP, the first thing I said was, 'You cannot do it alone. And we don't have all the answers.' That made the plan more human because, first of all, for the CEO to say, 'We don't have all the answers' is not natural. And, secondly, we cannot do it alone; the challenges are simply too big.

What we are trying to say is that society is the origin of business, of any business. Our business was created to solve a problem in society. The problems of hygiene in Victorian Britain were horrendous, so Lord Lever created soap for that reason, and the soap was successful because he responded to a need in society. Then he made money by doing that, which he then reinvested. He didn't do it to make money. That was an outcome, not a goal. And that is what you need to be sustainable. So if you put your business at the service of society and you really believe in that, not as a post-rationalisation, then you have unlimited growth opportunities as the challenges are still truly big. And, most importantly, you also have an unlimited acceptance by society.

It's actually amazing if you think about it. Creating a business model like this and creating movements around all of our brands, movements for good, giving all of our brands a deeper social purpose, is very much what business is all about. We see higher growth and profitability as a result and our share price as a consequence has done well. You could say that to some extent the financial sector has forgotten that social purpose, so they don't seem to value it that much. Quarterly profits seem to dominate and that guides the behaviour, unfortunately, of too many CEOs.

I believe personally, and we all in Unilever firmly believe, that if we continue to focus on servicing the needs of society and do that in a responsible way, our shareholders will also be better off.

Polman's strategy worked, driven by those Unilever brands like Lifebuoy, Dove, and Ben & Jerry's that "communicate a strong environmental or social purpose with products that contribute to achieving the company's ambition of halving its environmental footprint and increasing its positive social impact." These "Sustainable Living Brands" grew

69% faster than the rest of the business in 2019 and delivered 75% of the company's growth.[10] His focus on the needs of society certainly worked for the business and delivered Unilever's investors a Total Shareholder Return of 290% over his decade in charge.[11]

Alan Jope, Paul Polman's successor as Unilever CEO, has continued and even extended the company's commitment to doing well by doing good, as he explains in Chapter 6.

NOTES

1 http://davidsimon.com/festival-of-dangerous-ideas-2013.

2 Steinbeck, J. (1939). *The Grapes of Wrath*. Essex: Pearson Education, 2008: Chapter 5.

3 Danone (n.d.). A vision of Danone's role. http://ecosysteme.danone.com/danone-ecosystem-fund/genesis-and-mission/a-vision-of-danone-s-role.

4 Nike (n.d.). Nike aims to transform manufacturing. http://news.nike.com/pages/transform-manufacturing.

5 Klein, P. (2014, 4 December). In the future, companies will survive only if they help solve big social problems. *Forbes*. http://www.forbes.com/sites/forbesleadershipforum/2014/12/04/in-the-future-companies-will-survive-only-if-they-help-solve-big-social-problems/#22e840835f51.

6 Nike (2010). *Corporate Responsibility Report FY 07 08 09*. http://s3.amazonaws.com/nikeinc/assets/34527/Nike_FY07_09_CR_report.pdf?-1413902874.

7 *Financial Times* (2013, 28 January). Q&A: Coca-Cola chief Muhtar Kent. *Financial Times*. http://www.ft.com/cms/s/2/5d114ed2-5fff-11e2-b657-00144feab49a.html#axzz4AogEDhBx.

8 Skapinker, M (2010, 22 November). Corporate plans may be lost in translation. *Financial Times*.

9 Collins, J. C. (2001). *Good to Great: Why Some Companies Make the Leap... and Others Don't*. USA: William Collins.

10 https://www.unilever.com/news/press-releases/2019/unilevers-purpose-led-brands-outperform.html.

11 https://markets.ft.com/data/announce/full?dockey=1323-13884382-46HV22K0UH94PFI5VHO63DP2NM.

3

HOW SUSTAINABLE BRANDS ARE WINNING ON WALL STREET

As we saw in Chapter 2, Paul Polman set out his stall at the beginning of his decade as CEO of Unilever by telling investors that the company was moving in a pro-social, pro-environmental direction – that Unilever was going to become the ultimate sustainable corporate brand – whether they liked it or not:

> If you buy into this long-term value-creation model, which is equitable, which is shared, which is sustainable, then come and invest with us. If you don't buy into this, I respect you as a human being, but don't put your money in our company.[1]

Back in 2010, Polman was having to make the case to investors that rekindling and nurturing the link between business and society made business sense. He was having to do this because the investment community was not understood to be instinctively interested in companies focussing on anything other than the bottom line. "Doing good" was not something that featured large in quarterly investor and analyst calls. They may have asked questions about whether the company's risk profile was too high in supply chains or environmental impacts, but not about whether the company had a purpose or its brand was sustainable. Until now.

This change has been one of the most significant developments in the five years since this book was first published.

In 2018, Larry Fink, the chief executive officer of BlackRock, the world's largest asset manager with $6.5 trillion in assets under management, caused raised eyebrows among analysts and cheers among

DOI: 10.4324/9781003176817-3

campaigners, when he said in his annual letter to the companies his firm invests in (of which there are a lot) that

> Without a sense of purpose, no company, either public or private, can achieve its full potential. It will ultimately lose the license to operate from key stakeholders. It will succumb to short-term pressures to distribute earnings …, it will remain exposed to activist campaigns that articulate a clearer goal …. And ultimately, that company will provide subpar returns to the investors.[2]

The New York Times said, "It may be a watershed moment on Wall Street, one that raises all sorts of questions about the very nature of capitalism."[3]

Fink followed it up in his 2019 letter by saying,

> Profits and purpose are inextricably linked. Profits are essential if a company is to effectively serve all of its stakeholders over time – not only shareholders, but also employees, customers, and communities. Similarly, when a company truly understands and expresses its purpose, it functions with the focus and strategic discipline that drive long-term profitability […] Companies that fulfil their purpose and responsibilities to stakeholders reap rewards over the long-term. Companies that ignore them stumble and fail.[4]

So, just as Unilever discovered, a strong connection with society and understanding of the responsibility a company holds to the environment, are good for business. Investors like BlackRock are turning to companies with solid ESG (environmental, social, and governance) credentials not because they have a burning love for businesses that do good, not because they're hankering after a greater sense of purpose and meaning in their work, not because they suddenly want to save the world. But because it makes for better returns on their investments, and their traditional financial models were no longer assessing these risks and opportunities adequately.

BlackRock's turn to purpose and wanting to invest in companies who understand and act on their environmental and social obligations and opportunities is underpinned by research that ESG funds will account for almost 60% of mutual fund assets by 2025.[5] Many investors – public pension funds in particular – will not invest in companies without a clear and credible purpose, while increasing numbers of private equity firms are appointing heads of ESG to assess and manage their investees' performance in this space.

Whether passive or active, investors are encouraging companies to improve their social and environmental performance. Why? Because they have watched, researched, analysed, and interrogated companies' performance (more than any protester, regulator, or activist citizen was ever able to do) and come to the conclusion that companies who are not acting on their material environmental and social impacts represent too risky an investment.

Frank Cooper sits on the Executive Board at BlackRock as chief marketing officer and has seen at first hand the changing expectations on business from society and from investors like his firm. In an interview for this book, he gave his perspective on why this is happening.

> What I've seen in the past five years is an evolution from CSR to putting the question of how a business contributes to society in a positive way into the operation of the business. That to me is the idea of real purpose, of a deeper type of purpose and I think the seeds of that were planted a long time ago. We saw Occupy Wall Street and the whole concept of battling against the one-percenters and this basic sense that people were feeling left out of the prosperity that they saw fewer and fewer people enjoying.
>
> In the past, businesses could proceed under this idea of benevolence on the side, but not making it part of the corporation. But what we've seen in the past several years – and accelerated in the last two years – is a greater pressure against businesses directly and a greater awareness among the general public about the role of corporations in society. There's been a kind of awakening around the belief that corporations need to play a positive role and that there's no guarantee that any corporation has a licence to operate.
>
> On the social side, it's coming from the sense of growing inequality across the globe. You can see it politically probably more clearly in the populist movement. It's all over the world, where

there seems to be a growing gap in terms of wealth and income and a growing gap in a sense of opportunity among large groups of people. That has accelerated and created greater intensity around it.

On the environmental side, I think there is much better organisation around the globe. NGOs have become better marketers, better communicators, better thinkers and as a result have persuaded larger sections of the population that climate risk is real."

We've seen that at BlackRock specifically, we've seen protesters, letters, investors requiring us to pay closer attention to things like climate risk and as I talk to businesses across the globe, they are all sensing a greater awareness among the community and among the general public about the role corporations play. So, I've seen it and the intensity around that, but also a change in the type of awareness of what a corporation should do and the role it should play within a society.

This then leads to changes in how BlackRock assesses and chooses where it invests:

We approached it not purely from the angle that it's just the right thing to do. We took it from the perspective that climate risk is an investment risk and there is a fiduciary duty, no matter what your personal feelings might be about climate risk, to act. If you look at the data, it would suggest that that risk is only going to increase and that you would advise your clients to invest accordingly.

This new mindset from investors like BlackRock can drive change directly and indirectly:

A large portion of BlackRock's investments come through ETFs (Exchange Traded Funds) and Index Funds and so we're buying the entire market, but we think we still have a voice and an obligation to speak with management and use our voting power to make sure that management is heading down the right direction in the way we think protects our investors best. So, it's first and foremost through having the dialogue with the leadership within these various companies, but it's also our voting power that we use.

There's another lever that we've pulled and it's probably less obvious: we think our scale allows us to have a voice in the marketplace, so through thought leadership and through publishing articles and producing material to try to educate the broad investment community. We actually think that has a lot of weight and probably the most prominent of that is Larry's letter to CEOs, which he issues every year. It wasn't that what he said was new, it was the seat he was sitting in, at the heart of financial services, asset management and investment management, saying that this is absolutely necessary. The good news is that it does have an impact on the way that business leaders think, and also on other investors. We can increase the right kind of pressure and nudge people down the right path by pulling these levers.

Almost universally you hear leaders say they want to do things that actually have a positive impact on society. It's a reason they're in business, yes to make a profit for sure, but they believe that the products that they sell, or the services that they provide are in some way making life better for people. But it's the quarterly earnings pressure that they have difficulty balancing and it's understandable. And one of the great things about Larry's letters was that the theme throughout, probably at least the past five to six years, was that it's about having a long-term perspective and shifting away from the short termism that will actually prevent you from doing those things that will lead to the positive changes that society is expecting.

The environmental side has become so prominent in recent years, the pressure, the news coverage, the social media conversations around it have been front and centre. But you get a varying response when you talk to businesses about climate change and climate risk and usually it's around the pace of change and the need for them to do anything today. It depends on which industry that you're in; if you're in the energy sector you feel a little bit differently about it. You'll see some companies like BP, I think, taking a really strong and aggressive position on energy transition and so they're at the forefront of it.

When you get to the social issues there's less of an understating of what is the exact problem, because there is so much crammed into that, from inequality to LQBTQ rights, to labour rights and labour laws. As a result, it's difficult for people to compare across companies who's doing what and how successful they are. My approach to it has been that while we're in this period of time, pick something. You can start with whatever negative externality you think your business is causing and address it. Or you can pick something that you think your business is uniquely qualified to deliver against. But pick something. What I don't think is acceptable is the idea that, because there's this kind of nebulous nature to the S in ESG, that you can just idly sit by and wait till things clear up. Businesses will be held accountable.

I see purpose as an organising principle that unifies all stakeholders. If you look at it from the employees perspective, the best talent want to feel like the companies that they're working for are making a positive contribution to society and so where we stand in terms of environment, where we stand on social issues become important for that reason. If you didn't believe anything else, we know that's true.

We hear it in all the interviews and it's really surprised me at the extent we're hearing it. In virtually all the interviews they want to know how we're making a positive contribution, what's our view on the role of financial services and asset management in making the world a better place. What's interesting also is that we're hearing it from existing employees. They're not looking for some fancy statement or an eloquent phrase, they're looking for a pragmatic understanding of the ways in which the operating model of the company contributes to something positive in the world. So yes, the data shows that across interviews with external candidates and internal poll surveys, people want companies to have more of a purpose.

The second part is that we want the goodwill of the communities in which we operate and one of the trends is that there's kind of a deglobalisation – where people are feeling like they want to have more local presence and if you look at all the trust surveys they say that people are trusting those closest to them geographically, and so for us having a presence in the community and demonstrating that we're making a positive contribution in the community is also a benefit and we think that it plays into our social licence to operate. So, beyond risk there are definitely other reasons why we believe in ESG.

The investment community's increased focus on purpose and sustainability and the shift of ESG from niche interest to mainstream criteria underlines how clear to investors the link between business, society, and environment is, and they are starting to act accordingly. Chapter 4 explores where those links are and where commercial benefits can be found.

NOTES

1 Skapinker, Michael (22 November 2010). Corporate plans may be lost in translation. *Financial Times*.

2 https://www.forbes.com/sites/peterhorst/2018/01/16/blackrock-ceo-tells-companies-to-contribute-to-society-heres-where-to-start/?sh=-15c63310971d.

3 https://www.nytimes.com/2018/01/15/business/dealbook/blackrock-laurence-fink-letter.html.

4 https://www.blackrock.com/americas-offshore/en/2019-larry-fink-ceo-letter.

5 https://www.institutionalinvestor.com/article/b1qcg33v33y7zl/The-Pressure-Is-on-Private-Equity-To-Take-ESG-Seriously.

THE COMMERCIAL BENEFITS OF A SOCIAL MISSION

Our work at salt over the last 20 years has given us an inside view of how multinational companies have succeeded by realigning their businesses more closely with society. They have done this as the definition of society has expanded thanks to globalisation and digital connectivity and have managed to combine long-term thinking with short-term performance.

How have they done this? How do businesses benefit from realigning with society and promoting a social mission? In our experience, they win competitive advantage in four key areas:

a   Awareness and preference
b   Reputation and licence to operate
c   Innovation and market development
d   Employee engagement and talent acquisition

A. AWARENESS AND PREFERENCE

The biggest advertising budgets in the world belong to the owners of fast-moving consumer goods (FMCG), the personal and household necessities we buy every day from supermarkets without spending much time thinking about them in the shopping aisle. Procter & Gamble, the owner of brands like Crest toothpaste, Pantene shampoo, and Pampers nappies, spent upwards of $10 billion on advertising in 2018.

The marketing of these FMCG brands – the toothpastes and toilet rolls, soaps and shampoos – aims to persuade us not only that they "wash whiter" or "last longer" but also that these brands are

DOI: 10.4324/9781003176817-4

chosen by "people like us." And these messages need constant repetition because, unlike cars or smartphones, we're making choices between them and their competitors every week, so brand loyalty needs constant protection.

However, life is getting more difficult for these businesses and their brands. We might still be consuming their products in the same way, but we aren't consuming media like we used to. Gone are the days when a Persil ad in the UK during Coronation Street could reach 20 million people, over a third of the population. Brand owners relied on programmes like these to reach their consumers, and the support for them in the early days by companies like Procter & Gamble and Colgate Palmolive gave the programmes their name: soap operas or soaps.

Because we now consume media in such a different way, brand owners are having to find new ways to reach us and persuade us to consume their products. Recording programmes to watch later or downloading content from non-broadcasters means we can fast-forward through the ads or avoid them altogether. Dilemma number one for the FMCG brands.

The second problem is an increasingly diminishing return from traditional product innovation. How much whiter can our laundry get? How many more blades do we need on our razors? A slimmer innovation pipeline gives fewer new features to talk about in advertising to try and get the brand noticed. And, because media fragmentation makes it more difficult to reach consumers all at once, it has become more expensive to talk about separate innovations to them. From Coca-Cola to Kellogg's, companies are having to move towards a more holistic, "masterbrand" approach to their marketing, talking about the brand as a whole rather than specific brand variants.

The third challenge is the shift in the balance of power towards the retailers.

The rise of the mega retailers – Walmart employs 1% of Americans; £1 in every seven spent in the UK went through Tesco's tills at its peak; Carrefour has more than 12,000 stores around the world – has increased the pressure on FMCG manufacturers. They need their products not only to be on-shelf of these retailers but to be on-shelf prominently, so they have a better chance of being seen and selected in the few seconds of consideration a shopper gives to their choice of margarine or bleach.

This represents a significant cost of doing business. Trade spending (paying for position and prominence in retailers) accounts for 61% of a typical FMCG manufacturer's marketing budget and represents about 16% of gross sales, according to IBM's Institute for Business Value.[1]

This is one area where linking business more directly with society offers clear commercial opportunities. Owners of FMCG brands are finding that linking their brands more closely to a social cause – giving them a social mission – is helping them tackle each of these three problems.

Case study: Domestos

Domestos is a well-established household cleaning brand, sold in 35 countries (known in some of them by other names including Domex and Vim) and best known for "killing all germs dead" in the toilet.

The brand was launched in the UK in the 1920s and as a germ-killer had supported various public health campaigns, including encouraging polio vaccination in the UK in the 1950s. In 2012, although Domestos sales were good, the brand team were asking themselves all three questions noted above: how could they make their consumer communications less dependent on TV advertising? How could they communicate a "masterbrand" story (talking about Domestos as a whole, rather than relying on "new improved" innovations)? And how could they get prominent placing and support in-store without spending even more money on retailer promotions?

The answer lay in rediscovering the brand's social context and building a social mission, which was the task set before the global brand team at Domestos, their agencies (MullenLowe, their global advertising agency, who had created the "kill all germs dead" campaigns, and salt), and the in-house experts from parent company Unilever's Sustainable Living Plan team.

As a germ-killer located in the toilet, the team quickly identified the global sanitation crisis as a natural social issue for Domestos to tackle.

Worldwide, 2.5 billion people have inadequate sanitation and, of them, one billion practise open defecation. As a global issue, it is high on the agenda of the United Nations and organisations like the Bill & Melinda Gates Foundation. Beyond the personal indignities, inadequate sanitation reduces girls' attendance at school, puts women at risk of violence, reduces nutritional intake and increases stunting, and has severe economic impacts, costing India, for example, 6.4% of its GDP.[2] It is also an issue that people don't like to talk about: one of the reasons that sanitation lagged furthest behind its target among all the Millennium Development Goals in 2015 when they were replaced by the Sustainable Development Goals.

Domestos as a brand has no responsibility to tackle this crisis. But it does have an opportunity. Helping provide people with better access to sanitation creates a future market for Domestos, putting the brand in prime position to take advantage of any market growth.

The brand and agencies team were explicit about this from the outset: that engaging in the sanitation crisis was part of the brand's long-term growth strategy, not a short-term act of social responsibility or philanthropy. It was business realigned to the social context, not a social programme for nice PR.

We decided to link Domestos to this relevant social issue – poor sanitation – and use it to address these three business issues: the need for communications that didn't always rely on TV advertising; a broader brand story that didn't rely on constant innovations; and a way to gain shelf space in-store that didn't rely on increasing trade promotion fees to retailers.

Unilever therefore formed a partnership with UNICEF, to be led by the Domestos brand. This would help fund UNICEF sanitation initiatives and, in return, Domestos would be able to feature the UNICEF logo on-pack at certain times of the year.

The commitment enabled us to talk about a subject of genuine social concern and interest – certainly something of greater interest to journalists, bloggers and social media users than the efficacy of toilet bleach – and so boost Domestos's "earned media" coverage alongside its paid advertising. In year one of the campaign, this earned media reached nearly 16 million adults with universally positive messages, and allowed Domestos to explore new digital channels for communication.

The fact that this social mission was so intrinsically linked to the core of Domestos (its "masterbrand") meant our communications were able to have a direct, positive impact on its "brand equity" (how FMCG companies typically measure the effectiveness of communications). The campaign saw an increase from 12.5% to 16% in the perception that Domestos offers something that other brands do not, and an increase from 35% to 38% in Domestos's appeal compared to other brands.

Finally, the campaign led to increased shelf space and in-store support in partner retailers and corresponding increases in sales.

Why did retailers (Sainsbury's in the UK, for example) support this campaign? One of the key factors in people deciding where to shop (alongside proximity and price) is wanting to choose a retailer that "shares my values," where "people like me" shop. Retailers can demonstrate their values to shoppers in one of two ways: through their own community initiatives, and by giving prominence in-store to brands that also communicate those values.

People weren't setting off on shopping trips determined to choose Domestos because of its sanitation campaign. But they were, at least in part, making their choice of retailer based on shared values, and, once there, felt good about choosing a brand that espoused similar values, especially when it was featured prominently in-store. So Sainsbury's gave prominence to Domestos displays and shoppers bought more Domestos.

This fits with all the surveys that reveal the gap that exists between people's vague agreement that they want to do the right thing (save the planet, help good causes) but don't actually go out of their way to do anything about it. In this instance, shoppers were able to satisfy their underlying desire to "do the right thing" by shopping at a store that "shares my values" and selecting a brand that did the same, without having to make a special effort to seek it out or compromise on efficacy.

The results spoke for themselves, with Domestos sales increasing by 54%.

And, because this is a social mission, not simply a piece of cause-related marketing, it's not something that's going to stop. It will need to evolve as the social context evolves, but it's a long-term play.

Since that first UNICEF campaign, the brand has launched programmes like the Domestos Toilet Academy in India to train and support sanitation entrepreneurs; Clean Team in Ghana in partnership with Water and Sanitation for the Urban Poor to explore new models in urban areas; and school sanitation programmes in South Africa, Indonesia, and Vietnam.

Madhu Rao is Unilever's EVP for Home and Hygiene, the category that includes Domestos. He describes how the programme has come to define the brand.

As of 2020, Domestos has been able to provide access to safe sanitation to 28 million people across the world, a number that we are proud of and that we want to grow multiple times going forward. For example, our partnership with UNICEF has been ongoing and has met with very good success, targeting the neediest communities, especially rural. We're now looking to repeat that success in other markets with a focus on Africa.

When it comes to poor sanitation, school going children are most vulnerable. Globally, 40% of primary schools don't have access to safe sanitation so we're zeroing in on that issue through our school contact programmes in many countries. Our activities are global covering India, South Africa, Vietnam, Philippines, Turkey, Romania and Hungary to name a few.

At the same time, Domestos has been one of the fastest growing brands in Unilever and I strongly believe in the connection and that the right way to go about purpose is to support incredible programmes on the ground and talk about those in our consumer communications. To link 'brand do' and 'brand say'. Only then is purpose authentic and credible.

And the key to doing good and doing well is linking the product to the purpose. Domestos' product truth – the destructible force that kills all germs and viruses, the unstoppable force – is the reason why we are providing safe sanitation on the ground in our programmes. There's a great product-purpose fit and through that we've been able to create some very powerful communications.

Because of these actions, we have brought 'talkability' to a low-profile category like toilets and we've had fabulous support from customers, both modern trade retailers as well as general trade customers in our markets. We partner with traders in markets like India, Indonesia and Vietnam in our programmes because they are very influential in decision-making and they can spread awareness around improved sanitation.

Another benefit is that 'A' list celebrities from the Indian film industry have been inspired by our programme and are partnering with us in speaking up about sanitation and toilet cleaning, something you'd never have got before. Toilet cleaning is still seen as a taboo, even in big cities, let alone rural areas. The message that they have endorsed says everyone has a responsibility and duty to clean toilets, and it's not something that should fall to certain sections of society. We've seen more men cleaning toilets as a result of this campaign, which shows how it is helping unstereotype the issue.

> Our social mission has also driven innovation. One insight we found in India was that a liquid cleaner isn't so suited to the squat toilets that are standard there. So we created a powder format toilet cleaner, which can be sprinkled round and mixed with water for great results. The fact that it stays in place and is affordable means that it is getting very wide distribution now.
>
> Toilet cleaning going up is good business for us as well as good for society, and that's how our purpose is really working for us.

As well as its own work and partnerships, Domestos helped create the Toilet Board Coalition, a global, business-led coalition of companies, government agencies, sanitation experts, and non-profit organisations to develop sustainable and scalable solutions to the sanitation crisis. This coalition has brought together technologies, expertise, financial resources, and networks to build market-based sanitation initiatives that can be implemented sustainably at scale.

Also in this coalition are Kimberly-Clark (manufacturer of, among other things, Andrex, the toilet tissue and the UK's biggest non-food brand) and Lixil (owner of American Standard and Grohe, and the world's biggest manufacturer of toilets and sanitary fittings). All three companies have a clear vested interest in improved sanitation in the world to create new markets for their products and are aligning their businesses more closely to this broader social context.

In the quest for awareness and preference, businesses are finding that a social mission enables them to create distinctive, bold mass media campaigns that cut-through product-only stories; to communicate strong, positive messages about their brands in a way that is interesting to society and therefore interesting to the gatekeepers of "earned media" – the journalists, bloggers, commentators, and celebrities who make the news and light up social networks. They are finding that choosing the right social mission enables them to communicate the core essence of their brand. And they are finding that supporting the right social causes lets them demonstrate shared values with their retail customers and consumers.

For Domestos, that purpose is the elimination of germs and the diseases they spread, by cleaning toilets in developed countries and promoting better sanitation in developing ones.

When Nike ran a 2018 campaign featuring NFL star Colin Kaepernick, who had been shunned by teams after he had refused to take the knee during the playing of the national anthem – "Believe in something. Even if it means sacrificing everything" – they generated a huge amount of awareness, with media and public violently for and against it.[3]

The campaign resulted in consumer boycotts by people on one side of the issue, and a rush to buy Kaepernick shirts by people who supported his stance. The business result was one-sided though, with Nike's value reported as having increased by \$6 billion in the months following the campaign.[4]

It's difficult to assign that growth just to an ad campaign, but the campaign clearly had a lasting effect. Why? Because it associated the brand with a topical issue? No. It worked because it was entirely in tune with Nike's core purpose – to unite the world through sport to create a healthy planet, active communities and an equal playing field for all.

As far back as the 1970s Nike understood its social context and promoted its business by addressing relevant social issues in a way that could benefit the business. Gender equity was one such issue, linked to its business strategy of wanting to sell more sportswear to women. Nike demonstrated its active interest with early support of Title IX legislation in the US. Title IX was enacted in 1972 and states that "No person in the United States shall, on the basis of gender, be excluded from participation in, be denied the benefits of, or be subjected to discrimination under any education program or activity receiving federal financial assistance."[5]

By championing the legislation from the outset and supporting ongoing lobbying to keep it strong – in partnership with organisations like the Women's Sports Foundation, National Women's Law Center, and the NCAA (National Collegiate Athletic Association) – Nike sent a clear message to women throughout the US that it not only shared their values but was doing something about it.

Female participation in high school sports has increased by 940% since 1972[6] and Nike's women's range now accounts for approximately 25% of its business, with the company clear in its ambition to grow its business through investing further in women.[7]

As Nike's business has grown globally, the company has taken its mission more widely, not only through marketing communications inspiring women to "just do it" (celebrated in films like Voices, released in 2012 to mark the 40th anniversary of Title IX and featuring successful female athletes offering inspiration to the next generation)[8] but also through its creation of The Girl Effect in 2008, to raise awareness of the importance of the role of girls in international development.[9]

Our research of the post-Millennials – "Generation Z," born since 1995 – points to this trend of consumer businesses embracing social missions only growing, not least because of consumer demand for it.[10] 60% of the 16- to 20-year-olds we surveyed in the US, the UK, and Singapore said they would go out of their way to buy products and services from businesses they know are helping to create a better world. As observed in the Domestos example, there has traditionally been a gap between what people say they will do in surveys and what they actually do in practice, but the research did ask if they would "go out of their way" to buy responsibly. Further, three-quarters of those surveyed (74%) agreed that businesses should make "doing good" a central part of their business, and not just by giving to charity.

Being seen to be championing social issues that resonate with consumers and influencers enables brands to communicate their "brand essence" more effectively in an age of media fragmentation, too. Buying up airtime across so many different media to reach all of a brand's audiences is increasingly expensive. Espousing a cause that those audiences want to share to demonstrate their own values – getting them to do your job for you – is much cheaper. Think of the cost value equation for Patagonia every time a Gen Z shares a selfie wearing their jacket to show that they also care about the planet, let alone the free endorsement.

This move towards brands establishing and communicating a higher, social purpose is only getting stronger. Indeed, 78% of marketing directors felt that brand purpose has become more important as a result of the disruption to society in 2020.[11] The same report also advised brands to "think acts, not ads" and ensure that what they do is authentic to the brand and makes a tangible, measurable impact, just as Domestos and Nike have shown.

Alan Jope, the CEO of Unilever, observed this trend in an interview for this book, which features in Chapter 6:

> I think the way to consider this is, obviously I'm now generalising about big groups of populations, but as best we can tell, baby

boomers, which I avoid being by one year, don't even pretend to shape their purchase preferences based on environmental or social platforms. Gen X, which I guess I sneak into, we are worse because we lie. We say that we really care, but don't adjust our brand choices or behaviour very much at all. Gen Y/millennials are very motivated to change their behaviour to choose brands that are more sustainable, but only so long as it doesn't cost too much or is too inconvenient. But for Gen Z it is almost the only thing that's driving purchase behaviours. So if that kind of attitude is coming through the population like a pig through a python, it is a matter of remaining relevant into the future and securing the long-term health of the business that we take action on these issues. Millennials are no longer an adjunct; they're our core employee base and core target market.

It's not just consumer-facing businesses like Unilever that benefit from a social mission. Business-to-business companies, too, are finding that having one can drive their organisation forward; but for many of these it is licence to operate, market development, and employee engagement that are the bigger factors driving its adoption. These types of businesses often supply consumer-facing businesses anyway and are increasingly required through tenders and contracts to help fulfil the sustainability commitments of their customers.

B. REPUTATION AND LICENCE TO OPERATE

Reputation management was long seen as a dark art: managing issues to prevent bad news seeping out and getting in the way of maximising profits; building cosy relationships with regulators and politicians to ensure nothing too drastic happened to challenge the status quo; hiding from public view any practices that might damage a corporate reputation.

If that was once the way of going about it, it's almost impossible today. The internet has changed everything. It is,

an accelerator and force multiplier of opinions and perceptions. Indignation is its rocket fuel. When social media swerve against a popular personality, the traditional damage-control methods of well-greased PR machinery are usually no match for the stampede of screaming meemies.[12]

So too for businesses. Those that disappoint society's expectations and raise its indignation – by being seen to cheat workers, communities, the environment – are now much more likely to be found out. And that exposure goes very public, very quickly. Apps like DoneGood[13] and good on you[14] reveal the previously hidden shortcuts taken by businesses without due regard to the environmental or human cost of producing what they sell. And companies find it more difficult to treat their own workforces out of line with societal expectations when employee forums like Glassdoor make it easy to heap pressure and embarrassment on the company.

Tony Hayward famously lost his job as CEO of BP after the Deepwater Horizon oil spill. It is arguable he might have been able to keep his job, explain the spill as a terrible accident, and preserve BP's reputation – had he invested more in the company's licence to operate before the accident. However, he had made his approach clear in a speech to Stanford Business School in 2009, a year before the disaster, when he argued that BP had been going in the wrong direction before his appointment because it had "too many people that were working to save the world."[15] His position in relation to broader societal and environmental issues was clear, and the company's licence to operate in this new world more tenuous as a result.

The internet has given previously undreamt-of power to pressure groups like Greenpeace to expose "cheating," with highly effective campaigns that turn the marketing power of big brands back on their multinational owners in order to effect change. Its 2014 film targeting LEGO and Shell – *Everything is NOT Awesome*[16] – had five million views in its first month, drawing attention to Greenpeace's "Save the Arctic" campaign and putting pressure on LEGO to put pressure on Shell, a key retail partner for its toys.

A series of Greenpeace campaigns against Asia Paper and Pulp (APP), a company selling paper and packaging to other businesses, led to APP announcing a moratorium on all further forest clearance by its Indonesian suppliers. APP, as a business-to-business company, wasn't a household name and so had less to lose from consumers turning against them directly.

But these campaigns tapped into the power of societal expectations to impact business decisions by targeting the consumer-facing companies that were buying from APP, its B2B customers. One film targeting toy manufacturer Mattel featured its iconic Barbie doll being dumped by long-term boyfriend Ken when he discovered she was involved in deforestation.[17] A second, against KFC, featured Colonel "chainsaw" Saunders.[18] Both companies changed their paper sourcing policies as a result of the campaigns against them, leading to APP's own change of policy.

Greenpeace's parody of a Volkswagen ad featuring a small Darth Vader and attacking the company's environmental record resulted in over 520,000 people signing a petition against the company.[19] VW responded by agreeing to meet EU regulations to, among other things, cut CO_2 emissions by 2020, a piece of legislation the company had been lobbying against. Of course, VW's lack of real action and real commitment to reduce emissions eventually led to the emissions scandal of 2015 (when the company's licence to operate had already been weakened by the previous campaigns) with a resulting 25% drop in US sales year on year and a stock price fall to a record four-year low.

"Brand threat" can thus be applied to both business-to-business and business-to-consumer companies, as organisations like Green-peace bring the societal dimensions of a brand's actions to the attention either of consumers or of business customers via their consumers. Pressure is now applied through campaigners as well as through regulators, and increasingly investors too as we saw in Chapter 3.

Reputation is important to businesses because it affects their licence to operate. Where once this was determined by the small group of politicians and officials who regulated (or not) particular industries, the irreversible rise of social media has given a much more obvious and powerful social dimension to the question of licence to operate. Public pressure can now be applied to businesses where their practices don't conform to societal expectations, and their licence to operate is therefore much more closely related to public opinion. This broader social context is much more difficult to "manage" through individual relationships and traditional reputation management, the old dark arts.

Clothes manufacturers and retailers, for example, cannot afford to source from sweatshops in previously invisible corners of the world – or even to be unaware of what happens further down their supply chain – for fear of public "buycotts" hitting their business.

The only answer, as many consumer-facing businesses have discovered and more business-to-business businesses are discovering, is to do what society expects of them. Transparency makes the task of reputation management so much easier, too. To borrow from Mark Twain, "If you tell the truth, you don't have to remember anything."

So a business's licence to operate now depends disproportionally on its public reputation, and that public reputation is increasingly determined by what it does in practice across all its operations, not just what it chooses to communicate. The "do" has to match the "say."

Of all the industries for which reputation, regulation and licence to operate are important, agribusiness ranks among the highest. It is an industry that is highly regulated (by organisations like the Food and Drug Administration in the US and the European Food Safety Authority) and which has aroused huge pressure-group action and public suspicion dating back to the launch of GMO seeds in Europe in the 1990s and earlier. Questions of reputation and licence to operate are central to companies like BASF, Bayer Monsanto, Dow, and Syngenta, the biggest agrochemical businesses in the world.

Between 2008 and 2015, Mike Mack was CEO of Syngenta, a company formed in 2000 when Novartis and AstraZeneca merged their agribusinesses. In an interview in 2014 for the first edition of this book, he explicitly linked his company's growth to understanding the social context in which it operates.

> The company purpose is 'bringing plant potential to life.' We didn't ask the question, 'What are we doing here?' but, rather, 'What is the unique purpose of Syngenta?' Not what do we wish to become, but rather who are we actually already? And, if you look at our products and what motivates the science and our people around the world, bringing plant potential to life best encapsulated what we we're all about.
>
> It has embedded in that single phrase a huge amount of growth potential. By growth I do mean when you look at the number of crops that today aren't as bountiful as they could be, it unlocks a huge amount of opportunity: commercial opportunity, scientific opportunity and potential for our people to be involved in considering how to progress it. When you then translate that in to a global context – seven billion people becoming nine or ten – and the requirements that that's going to have on the

planet, why wouldn't you want to commit yourself to bringing plant potential to life?

Because, if we do it well, it will make perfectly good business sense, it will really motivate the people that work for us, and it will have a contribution to wider society, starting with the prosperity of farmers around the world who are directly our customers, and further into consumers and the multitudes of others involved in the food chain.

Syngenta was acquired by ChemChina in 2017, China's biggest ever foreign takeover at that time,[20] as it looked to improve domestic agriculture output.

From China to California, regulation is now catching up with this social licence to operate. Where Greenpeace mobilises campaigns against companies around their environmental impacts, so governments in turn build policy frameworks to regulate them. China has set out its goal to hit carbon neutrality by 2060[21]; the European Union has announced its plans to cut greenhouse gas emissions by at least 55% by 2030, on the way towards carbon neutrality by 2050[22]; and California Governor, Gavin Newsom, announced in 2020 that sales of gasoline-fuelled vehicles would be banned by 2035, as part of the State's own journey to carbon neutrality by 2045.[23]

The growth of ethical and green sales has encouraged more businesses to look to social purpose and sustainability as growth drivers. But regulation is now looking to shut the door on those wanting to overclaim. As noted before, businesses on a mission need to match what they say with what they do. The UK's Competition and Markets Authority (CMA) announced at the end of 2020 that it would be starting a new programme of work to vet business claims about the sustainability or environmental impact of their products,[24] targeting those companies who want to make the right noises without doing the right things.

C. INNOVATION AND MARKET DEVELOPMENT

When William Lever looked at the social context in which his business was operating – tens of thousands of people across the river in Liverpool living in overcrowded slum housing, with diseases like cholera and typhoid rife – he saw the opportunity for market development: that there were thousands, millions of people living in similar conditions across Britain who would benefit from access to soap (Louis Pasteur had proved the link between micro-organisms and infectious disease in the late 1850s and early 1860s, establishing the link between hygiene and public health).

But soap at the time wasn't generally affordable to the people who lived in Liverpool's slums, and wasn't sold as a health or hygiene product. Soap had primarily been a luxury product for the aspiring classes and taxed as such.

The social context pointed to a new market opportunity and drove Lever to innovation. He created Lifebuoy, a carbolic soap that was not only affordable to these new potential consumers but also named and marketed for its hygiene and health-promoting qualities.

Lever wasn't a cynical businessman. He had a genuine desire to better the lot of his fellow men (albeit in some ways that might look terribly paternalistic today). But the fact that he intertwined business and social mission so closely enabled him to create a brand in Lifebuoy that today, 130 years on, is the biggest health soap brand in the world and one that expanded its business even further during the pandemic by once again meeting society's needs.

Today, Lever's approach might be called "bottom of the pyramid" marketing, and the opportunities for businesses to develop new markets by meeting the needs of the poorest but largest socio-economic groups are extensively discussed and debated by management thinkers as well as business leaders, most notably *C.K. Prahalad in The Fortune at the Bottom of the Pyramid*.[25]

Lifebuoy soap is now a multinational business with the same social mission, albeit on a larger scale, to change handwashing behaviours and reduce the spread of infectious diseases.

Lifebuoy still looks to the social context for its market development. It is introduced to new countries today where there is the same need as existed in the slums of Victorian England: namely, for people to be able to learn the life-saving benefits of soap and afford to use it. Lifebuoy is the biggest soap brand in India and across much of South and South East Asia, and uses its social mission to reach new consumers every year across Asia, Africa, and Latin America.

Its social mission informs everything the brand does, from new product development to advertising and leadership development.

Its innovations are geared to preventing the spread of infectious diseases (including Covid-19) by encouraging people to wash their hands with soap more regularly. So their innovation pipeline produces ranges like a colour-changing hand wash[26] to encourage children to wash their hands more often and more thoroughly.

In the same way, organisations like Unilever, Kimberly-Clark, and Lixil see significant market development opportunities among the 2.5 billion people who do not have access to adequate sanitation. In improving sanitation for these people, the Toilet Board Coalition,[27] of which both are members, is likely to help create new markets for toilet cleaners, tissues and fittings. Tackling the social issue leads to the market opportunity.

The pharmaceutical industry has had a mixed relationship with social mission. Big Pharma has been labelled "Bad Pharma" and attacked in many forms (think *The Constant Gardener*[28]) for bad science, "buying" doctors and accusations of withholding drugs from those who can't afford them, notably antiretroviral medicine for HIV in Africa.

But more recent initiatives show how pharmaceutical companies are addressing social causes not to take the heat off or to manage their reputations, but rather to open up new markets – something that even their most vociferous opponents would recognise as likely to generate serious commitment from the industry.

GlaxoSmithKline (GSK) is the world's sixth biggest pharmaceutical company and had revenues of over £34 billion in 2020. In the 1990s and early 2000s, the firm came under attack from AIDS activists for refusing to allow the manufacture of cheap generic versions of their antiretroviral drugs in South Africa, because of the patents they had issued. The Competition Commission in South Africa found in 2003 that GSK (and another pharmaceutical company, Boehringer) had broken the law by refusing to license their patents to generic manufacturers in return for a reasonable royalty.

Since then, the firm has changed its approach, recognising the primacy of the social context to its business. In 2009, GSK established with Pfizer, the world's second biggest pharmaceutical business, an independent company focussed on the needs of people living with HIV. The new company, ViiV Healthcare, explicitly recognised the need to link the business more closely to society, with a stated aim: "to leave no person living with HIV behind"[29] and offers its antiretroviral drugs at not-for-profit prices to the World Bank's low-income countries and all of sub-Saharan Africa.

Later, in 2013, GSK announced a broader partnership with Save the Children to "share our expertise and resources with the aim of helping to save one million children's lives."[30] The partnership focusses on developing child-friendly medicines to reduce child mortality and new-born deaths; widening vaccination coverage to reduce the number of child deaths in the hardest-to-reach communities; increasing investment in the training, reach and scope of health workers in the poorest communities to help reduce child mortality; and researching new affordable nutritional products to help alleviate malnutrition in children.

Most notable at the time of the launch were the comments of the Chief Executive of Save the Children UK. He said that, in the past, Save the Children "may not have embarked on a collaboration with a pharmaceutical company like GSK" and that he himself had picketed outside the gates of the company over their role in keeping prices high for AIDS drugs. But now he felt that GSK had changed and was at the forefront of access to medicine and investment in malaria vaccines.[31]

And, just as the charity recognised the role a business like GSK could now play in pursuing their social goals around saving children's lives, so the business recognised the role this social mission – and partnerships with organisations like Save the Children – could play in its own long-term market development.

Sir Andrew Witty, then chief executive officer, had announced in 2009 that GSK would reinvest 20% of its profits from the Least Developed Countries (LDCs) back into those countries to support and develop healthcare. At the time it was reported that this wasn't just about giving, but also made commercial sense for GSK. Africa is a growing market, it needs drugs badly, and will gradually be able to buy more drugs as its economies develop.

In relation to the Save the Children partnership he said, "So [while] we've made it very clear that we are not looking to make a return from the source of these activities, we are equally not looking to make a loss – we need it to be sustainable."[32]

With its controversial history and issues relating to corruption, it's clear the pharmaceutical industry doesn't feel totally comfortable yet with talking about tackling social issues as a part of their business growth strategy. But it's equally clear that the two fit together. Help address Africa's societal needs today and build new markets for tomorrow.

The industry's response to the Covid-19 pandemic follows this pattern. AstraZeneca announced in June 2020 that it would not profit from sales of its vaccine while Covid-19 was considered a pandemic, before coming under pressure to clarify how it would decide when the pandemic was over.[33]

Big Pharma may struggle over how it balances commercial and societal interests, but of all the industries who operate in a societal context, they are surely among the most obvious.

D. EMPLOYEE ENGAGEMENT AND TALENT ACQUISITION

The Gallup Q12 survey is used to measure how engaged employees are at work. Over the last 20 years, 5.4 million people have been asked 12 simple questions that not only track how engaged they are in their work but also what drives that engagement. Most powerfully, the results have proved a direct correlation between employee engagement and business performance: higher employee engagement results in better performance; lower employee engagement results in worse performance.

Every two to four years, Gallup conducts a meta-analysis of these surveys and, in 2020, it conducted one covering just under 2.7 million employees from 276 organisations in 96 countries.[34]

It confirmed that across all these companies, all these countries, all these people, businesses or work units scoring in the top half on employee engagement more than double their odds of success compared with those in the bottom half. Think about that: an engaged workforce doubles the likelihood that a business will succeed.

However, Gallup's research showed that just 15% of workers are engaged at work. People spend an awful lot of their lives at work. That barely one in seven feel engaged in their work is dispiriting in itself. But it makes no business sense either.

One of the questions in the Q12 goes to the heart of the relationship between business and social mission. Respondents are asked to rate whether "The mission or purpose of my company makes me feel my job is important." Does a closer link between a business and the social context in which it is operating make for stronger employee engagement?

Unilever has a reputation for being at the forefront of how business can connect positively to social and environmental issues. In 2020, the GlobeScan – SustainAbility survey ranked it number one for corporate sustainability leadership for the tenth year in a row[35] and *The Economist* described the company as "generally reckoned to have the most comprehensive strategy of enlightened capitalism of any global firm."[36]

The way it structured its business around its social context, with its Sustainable Living Plan essentially the business strategy, not only delivered higher engagement among its employees (and better business results) but attracted new talent too: as the Sustainable Living Plan bedded in after its launch in 2010, the firm moved into the top three in LinkedIn's lists of the Most "InDemand" Employers in the world, alongside Google and Apple.[37]

Our Generation Z research pointed to a similar trend, with nearly 60% of 16- to 20-year-olds in the US and Singapore and 45% in the UK saying that in choosing a job they would rank working for a company that helps make the world a better place as important a consideration as salary.[38]

In the war for talent, having a social mission has become the weapon of choice for progressive businesses, and an essential ingredient for any business wanting an engaged workforce and the commercial advantages that brings.

NOTES

1 IBM (2003). *Play Big: The Consumer Packaged Goods Imperative.* http://globalscorecard.gs1.org/gsclive/download/G510_9137_03f_play_big_1.pdf.

2 Water and Sanitation Program, World Bank (2010). *Inadequate Sanitation Costs India Rs.2.4 Trillion (US$53.8Billion).* https://www.wsp.org/sites/wsp.org/files/publications/wsp-esi-india.pdf.

3 https://www.theguardian.com/sport/2018/sep/04/nike-controversial-colin-kaepernick-campaign-divisive.

4 https://www.vox.com/2018/9/24/17895704/nike-colin-kaepernick-boycott-6-billion.

5 Title IX, Education Amendments of 1972. https://www.dol.gov/oasam/regs/statutes/titleix.htm.

6 National Women's Law Center (2011). The Battle for Gender Equity in Athletics in Colleges and Universities. http://www.nwlc.org/sites/default/files/pdfs/2011_8_battle_in_college_athletics_final.pdf.

7 https://www.cnbc.com/2019/04/16/nikes-fix-for-boosting-sales-at-home-women.html

8 Nike (22 June 2012). Nike celebrates women in sport with 'Voices' film. http://news.nike.com/news/nike-women-in-sport-voices-film.

9 https://www.girleffect.org/

10 https://www.slideshare.net/sustainablebrands/generation-z-infographic.

11 https://content.ascential.com/rs/897-MBC-207/images/WARC_Marketers_Toolkit_2021.pdf.

12 Wolcott, James (9 January 2015). The Bill Cosby scandal, brought to you by YouTube. *Vanity Fair*. http://www.vanityfair.com/hollywood/2015/01/bill-cosby-hannibal-buress-youtube.

13 https://donegood.co/.

14 https://goodonyou.eco/.

15 Entrepreneurial spirit needed: Tony Hayward, British Petroleum, 27 July 2009. YouTube. https://www.youtube.com/watch?v=FwQM00clxgM.

16 LEGO: Everything is NOT awesome, 8 July 2014, YouTube. https://www.youtube.com/watch?v=qhbliUq0_r4.

17 Barbie's rainforest destruction habit REVEALED! 6 June 2011, YouTube. https://www.youtube.com/watch?v=Txa-XcrVpvQ.

18 Maharuddin, Rusmadya (31 May 2012). KFC's chainsaw colonel visits Indonesian rainforest destruction. *Greenpeace*. http://www.greenpeace.org.uk/blog/forests/kfcs-chainsaw-colonel-visits-indonesian-rainforest-destruction-20120531.

19 VW: The dark side, 27 June 2011, YouTube. https://www.youtube.com/watch?v=nXndQuvOacU.

20 https://www.reuters.com/article/us-syngenta-ag-m-a-chemchina-idUSKBN1810CU.

21 https://www.bbc.co.uk/news/science-environment-54256826.

22 https://ec.europa.eu/clima/policies/eu-climate-action/2030_ctp_en.

23 https://www.gov.ca.gov/2020/09/23/governor-newsom-announces-california-will-phase-out-gasoline-powered-cars-drastically-reduce-demand-for-fossil-fuel-in-californias-fight-against-climate-change/.

24 https://www.gov.uk/government/news/cma-to-examine-if-eco-friendly-claims-are-misleading.

25 Prahalad, C.K. (2004). *The Fortune at the Bottom of the Pyramid*. Pennsylvania: Wharton School Publishing.

26 https://www.unilever.com/news/news-and-features/Feature-article/2013/the-hulk-of-handwashes.html.

27 https://www.toiletboard.org/.

28 le Carré, John (2001). *The Constant Gardener*. London: Hodder & Stoughton. Also film of the same name (2005).

29 https://viivhealthcare.com/en-gb/about-us/our-culture-and-values/.

30 https://www.gsk.com/en-gb/about-us/save-the-children-partnership/.

31 BBC (10 May 2013). GlaxoSmithKline launches Africa charity partnership. http://www.bbc.co.uk/news/business-22476556.

32 BBC (10 May 2013). GlaxoSmithKline launches Africa charity partnership. http://www.bbc.co.uk/news/business-22476556.

33 https://www.reuters.com/article/uk-health-coronavirus-astrazeneca-contra-idUKKBN2841FA.

34 https://www.gallup.com/workplace/321725/gallup-q12-meta-analysis-report.aspx.

35 https://www.unilever.com/news/news-and-features/Feature-article/2020/global-experts-rank-unilever-no1-for-sustainability-leadership.html#:~:text=Next-,Global%20experts%20rank%20Unilever%20No.,the%20latest%20GlobeScan%2DSustainAbility%20survey.

36 *The Economist* (9 August 2014). Unilever: In search of the good business. http://www.economist.com/news/business/21611103-second-time-its-120-year-history-unilever-trying-redefine-what-it-means-be.

37 Raybould, James (16 October 2013). Unveiling LinkedIn's 100 Most InDemand Employers of 2013. LinkedIn. https://blog.linkedin.com/2013/10/16/unveiling-linkedins-100-most-indemand-employers-of-2013.

38 https://mullenlowesalt.com/tag/generation-z/.

5

WHAT MAKES A GOOD SOCIAL MISSION?

As we have seen, developing and communicating a social mission offers businesses multiple benefits and opportunities to create a more sustainable business model. But what does this look like?

We have found through our work over the last 15 years that a successful social mission typically exhibits six key characteristics:

1 **A**lignment to the overall corporate strategy
2 **S**trong link to the product or service
3 **C**lear commercial interest
4 **E**ncouragement for others to join
5 **N**arrative for the brand story
6 **D**river of engagement across the organisation

This **ASCEND** model makes it possible to identify whether a social mission can succeed in creating both business growth and social good.

1 **Alignment to the overall corporate strategy.** Lifebuoy's social mission to help people protect themselves from infection through increasing the habit of handwashing with soap, and Domestos's social mission to kill germs for good through improving access to sanitation are both easily connected to Unilever's overall vision to grow the business, decouple its environmental footprint from its growth and increase its positive social impact. Likewise, the Andrex social mission ("to bring the dignity of improved sanitation to all") fits neatly with the corporate

DOI: 10.4324/9781003176817-5

mission of its parent company, Kimberly-Clark, "to lead the world in essentials for a better life."

This is more than semantics. A corporate mission captures the growth strategy of a company and aligning a social mission to it ensures leadership support inside the company, something that is especially critical in the early days.

2   **Strong link to the product or service.** Not all connections are as obvious from the outset as the role of soap in promoting handwashing, or actually involve the company's product or service directly in their delivery. The acid test of a social mission is that nobody should have to think twice about why the company or brand is involved in this particular cause. So it is clear why banks might support financial literacy programmes in schools or among underprivileged groups, or why recruitment firms should support access to employment and social mobility schemes. It is less clear why the cosmetics company and soap shop Lush should tackle the issue of wrongdoing by undercover police as it did in its #SpyCops campaign in 2018, a campaign which it suspended in the face of public opposition and no little confusion.[1]

3   **Clear commercial interest**. As has been noted earlier, being transparent about the commercial vested interest is critical to the success of a social mission and ensuring it lasts. It forces the alignment of commercial and social goals, it builds transparency and trust among partners and third parties, and it ensures that the whole organisation can understand and support the social mission whether they believe in doing good, doing well or both. Not talking about the commercial aims of a social mission happens where people feel uncomfortable about talking about good causes and good profits in the same breath. They can feel uneasy bringing the two together and don't want to come across as hard-hearted and uncaring. The irony is that when companies say they're not in it for the money, outsiders simply don't believe them, which only serves to erode trust and damage their reputation.

Clarity about how it drives growth is perhaps the most critical factor to building momentum and energy behind a social mission in any organisation. This is human nature: people, however compassionate they are towards the plight of others, find it more difficult to sustain charity and empathy where there's nothing in it for them, a tendency described by the philosopher, Bertrand Russell: "Whatever is to be done can only be done adequately by the help of a certain zest, and zest is difficult without some self-regarding motive."[2]

4   **Encouragement for others to join in**. A social mission should attract other organisations to join as partners. By definition, a social mission should encourage the involvement of other actors in society. So, Lifebuoy's handwashing efforts attract the support of national and regional governments, NGOs like UNICEF and Oxfam, funding bodies like USAID and the Bill & Melinda Gates Foundation, as well as celebrities and the media. Global Handwashing Day has been enthusiastically supported and celebrated for many years by Lifebuoy on October 15th, a day now recognised by the UN. Lifebuoy runs Global Handwashing Day activities in all the countries where it sells, but the day is open to any organisation and materials are made freely available to encourage them to join in. Similarly, a good social mission encourages others to do your marketing job for you – everything from on-pack logos (like Andrex and UNICEF) and celebrity endorsements (as we saw with Bollywood stars and Domestos in Chapter 4) to people sharing Patagonia-hoodied selfies.

5   **Narrative for the brand story**. As discussed in Chapter 4, Section a, businesses are having to become more resourceful in how they go about telling their story to potential customers: customers who are no longer huddling around the same television programmes and who are becoming increasingly adept at avoiding or ignoring traditional advertising. Brands need a narrative that breaks through these defences and invites people to be interested in them. A good social mission provides a narrative for the brand story, something of genuine interest that is sufficiently connected to the brand to build affinity towards it. Importantly, brands have to talk about their social mission in the same voice and with the same brand personality as they talk about everything else.

Kenco's "Coffee vs Gangs" initiative did just this – use a social mission to enhance its brand narrative.[3] Kenco had well-established sustainable sourcing credentials, including a long-term partnership with the Rainforest Alliance and parent company Mondelez's "Coffee Made Happy" programme. Sustainable sourcing of coffee (minimising the environmental impacts and increasing positive social impacts in coffee-growing regions) is becoming a category norm and therefore more difficult to use as a competitive differentiator. "Coffee vs Gangs" told the story in a new way – how, as part of its sustainable sourcing strategy, Kenco was helping young men in Honduras turn away from gangs and towards building skills and careers in coffee farming. This new approach to communicating the social mission resonated with coffee consumers in key markets for Kenco like the US and UK, especially mothers who could empathise with the fear of sons being lured by gang culture and helped create a stronger brand narrative that reached beyond the constraints of paid-for advertising. This role for a social mission in creating a new jump-off point for creativity and mass media communication is becoming increasingly recognised by brands, like Knorr, one of the world's largest cooking brands, and its launch of Eat for Good in 2021.[4]

6 **Driver of engagement across the organisation.** As seen above, there is a direct correlation between employee engagement and business performance, and employees are increasingly expressing their preference to work for organisations with a meaningful purpose. The best social missions therefore create opportunities for employees to participate through their day jobs as well as through volunteering programmes.

If these are the characteristics of a successful social mission, how do organisations create them? Well, they don't create them, by and large. The best social missions are found, not created. They exist already in the company's history or founding principles, in the product design or brand essence, in customer relationships or consumer insights.

Nike discovered its social mission in the founding belief of Bill Bowerman and Phil Knight that everyone was an athlete whose performance could improve. As the company has grown, so has the social mission to ensure that everyone can fulfil their athletic potential regardless of gender or anything else.

Marks & Spencer found its social mission, communicated as Plan A, in its history and in its relationship with its shoppers. Plan A was lauded as exemplary of good corporate practice when launched in 2007 and illustrates well all six of the ASCEND characteristics. Adam Elman was global head of Plan A Delivery at the time of launch and described the evolution of Plan A and how it worked in practice in an exclusive interview for this book.

Adam Elman

The core values of M&S are Inspiration, Innovation, In Touch and Integrity. Sustainability sits under all of these in many different guises. I think you hear a lot of businesses that talk about this being ingrained in the DNA and that's actually a phrase we like a lot as M&S has a long track record of 'doing the right thing'.

If you go back to the founders of the business, their mission was very much about improving the quality of people's lives. That's what M&S was set up to do. Who those people are and what quality means, you can take in very many different ways. You can go back in the history books and in the 1930s M&S was a leading company in staff welfare and again with community investment in the 1990s. In 2007 M&S launched our eco/ethical plan, Plan A (because there is no Plan B for our one planet). If you like, it is a modern manifestation of what the business was doing for many years, with an even bigger desire to lead and drive forwards.

There are many retailers you can go and shop from nowadays, so why is it customers come to Marks & Spencer? Two very big reasons are quality and trust. People come to us because of our high quality and a lot of what sustainability delivers equals quality: whether that be Fairtrade, sustainable cotton, sustainably caught fish, high ethical standards or helping disadvantaged people get in to work – our customers trust and expect us to do the right thing.

Only a small percentage of M&S customers are 'green crusaders'; however, most of our customers want to do the right thing – they don't want to be preached at, but they do want and expect big businesses such as M&S to help them.

We launched our clothes recycling initiative 'Shwopping' in conjunction with Oxfam as a way to help our customers ensure garments they no longer want could be easily reused or recycled. The programme has been extremely successful with over 25 million garments having been donated, raising millions of pounds for Oxfam. At the time of launch, our brand measures on quality improved as customers people perceive that, if you are doing these things, you're going to be around for a long time: you're here for the future.

Partnerships have always been key to our progress. We have various charity partnerships in place and they are designed to work for the long term to deliver shared value for both partners. This principle of shared value is extremely important, and we're not embarrassed about the fact that it delivers and supports our business at the same time. We think what we do is fair and we're honest and transparent about our relationships.

Now that's not to say that everything we do as a business delivers an instant return to us. There are plenty of things we just have to invest in, things like sustainable timber or sustainable cotton. There are some things that are just the right thing to do and we're prepared to invest in them.

Everything we do supports building trust on an ongoing basis. Trust is an interesting thing. It takes many years to get and you can lose it in seconds. Through Plan A we have a robust plan and governance in place and, through our values, we're always working hard to ensure we maintain and build on this trust.

Manpower Group is in a different business sector and has operated in the world of work for nearly 70 years. Founded and headquartered in Milwaukee, Wisconsin, it places 3.4 million people in work each year, working with over 400,000 clients in 80 countries. In 2014 the company appointed the fourth (and first to be born outside of the US) CEO in its history, Jonas Prising from Sweden. He gave his views in an interview for this book on the relationship between his company and its societal context.

Jonas Prising

Our founders from the beginning had a view that we should not only run a very good business, but also make sure that we never lose sight of the fact that running a good business means contributing to society at large by providing meaningful and safe employment for millions of people.

So, we've had this duality of purpose within our organisation as part of our culture and as part of our ethos, frankly since the beginning, and well before discussions around sustainability came about. A stakeholder view as opposed to a shareholder view, where it made perfect sense to take this position as a corporation. We had this as an ingrained view of what the business is all about and maybe that came from the fact that our product is really in providing people, helping them do really well, and helping companies find and make the best match with talent that can immediately contribute to their organisation.

We connect with people who want to find a job for the first time, for the second time, coming back to work, people changing career, changing direction, or who have never been employed, having been long-term unemployed, trying to make some form of transition. We are at the bleeding edge of people wanting to change their situation one way or another so that they can lead a better life. That is why they come here.

Our founder [Elmer Winter] talked about this internally to our organisation, back in 1969, that you should never forget that the work that you do is really important to people and what matters in people's lives and that you're making a very important contribution by enabling them to join the labour market in the course of your daily activities.

At the time, he was very keen to implant within our culture this notion that to do well in a business you have to be part of a community. So, very early on, I think he had an understanding that taking this view was going to be beneficial to the business. People will want to come and work for you, which means the business is going to do well.

There are many worthwhile causes in life. There are so many good things that we can do and that we all do in one way or another in a personal capacity. But, from an organisational perspective, what we are determined to support are things that are related to improving people's lives through work and providing meaningful work. That means that we are very active in preparing young people for their entry into the workforce.

So, activities that relate to education for young people are important to us. We can provide programmes in line with that. We can provide programmes for people who are disabled or long-term unemployed and be a gateway for them to enter the workforce. If disaster strikes – like the 2004 Asian tsunami – we may send funds to the Red Cross, but we're more likely to do things that can help people get back on their feet by acquiring a skill or being in a position to acquire a skill so that they can feed their families through work. We did that in India and helped women learn trades that helped rebuild their communities and bring money back to their families. That's our core strength and core capability.

We try to have a very tight connection between what we do as a business and how we intend to do good in the community that we serve. Otherwise, what you tend to see are companies supporting things that they sort of like, that the CEO likes, and that is when I think you see a divergence in the focus of the organisation, or it means values turn into fads when people move on.

We do know that this is something that the world at large increasingly expects and will expect from organisations such as ours. Our whole mission in life is not just to provide value to shareholders: we have to provide value to our employees, we have to provide value to the communities in which we are active, and we have to make – and we want to make – a meaningful contribution to improving the working lives of as many people as we can.

Our clients see that, recognise that and appreciate that. In that sense, they view it as positive, and it can give us a commercial benefit. We are not doing it to position ourselves in a particular way; we're doing it because we believe it's the right thing to do and it's part of our mission to achieve those kinds of objectives as well as our financial objectives.

The other extreme are the people who feel that it is not necessarily the right thing to do, but the right thing to talk about. So people are talking and making all kinds of contortions as to why the product or the service they provide is improving lives. They have to go for derivatives that are five or six steps away: 'if you do this, fewer people will die, there'll be less deforestation in the Amazon' and so on. That may be true by the way, but I'm just happy that we have a very short jump between what we do as a business and our contribution to society.

We celebrate that internally, of course; we have it front and centre in terms of who we are. This is a highly volatile environment and it's difficult to predict where people and organisations are going to be. So the one thing that I can guarantee with certainty is that the core foundations, our values, stay the same. We may be moving into different countries, we may be adding business lines, we may be divesting business lines, and we may do many things as an organisation so that we can better serve our clients and candidates. But the core foundation of who we are and what we believe stays the same.

When you join our organisation there are some things you can count on. You know that we're an ethical company. You know we truly believe in doing good while doing well. And, if you sign up to that and if you think that's important, you're more likely to stay with us for a long time. You're more likely to be more engaged, and, if you're more engaged and passionate about what you do, you are going to be providing a better service to our clients. I guess also we are fortunate because the link between motivated, well-trained and engaged employees and a better business result is pretty clear for us: you're going to find employees being more engaged when they work with job seekers and when they talk to clients.

[Partnerships with NGOs] depend on which organisations you work with. Those more influenced by government institutions tend to be less performance-oriented and metric-driven. It's much easier for us to relate to and work with organisations that have defined outcomes and measure results in some form or fashion, and that's the way we're increasingly expecting NGOs to operate. I have seen the shift just in my being a member of the Junior Achievement organisation for the last 15 years. Donors have become much more sophisticated. They want to know what they're donating for you to do, and how you'll know when you've achieved it.

I think that is a very big shift in terms of how NGOs are being forced to operate to raise funds. As corporations become more involved, they will expect a return, not in financial terms, but in graduation rates improving, for example, and by how much, because there may be somebody else who is going to be 10% better. Those more inclined in that way are easier for us to work with because it's easier for business, but I don't think that's unique to us.

As a European now living in the US, I notice the differences. Europe is, in a way, more communal with the "greater good" mind-set, and you see that reflected in how we built society in Europe. Yes, we all pay higher taxes, but we do think that those taxes go to something good such as education, free healthcare, all of those things. We understand the bigger obligation.

Now the American view would that be by doing and acting in my own self-interest 'I will maximise the opportunities', which in the end will benefit the greater good as well. If I do well, I'm going to pay more taxes and people will be better of fall around. But the US view is now shaped a little bit more by the importance of being a good corporate citizen in more ways than just a shareholder view. Americans are very pragmatic. I think the US is adding a dimension to its thinking around the contributions that you make to society as an individual and as an organisation. It's a much more engaged model.

The evidence of the need for a bigger role [in society] – or at least an awareness of the bigger role – is there. Younger people expect it. If you're recruiting talent into your organisation, they have expressed a desire for greater meaning to what it is they do.

At this point I don't think it's self-preservation from the company perspective, but consumers appreciate companies that do the right thing, employees want to work in companies that do the right thing, and therefore we're going to run our business in that way because it makes a difference in so many aspects.

All businesses interact with society, impact the environment, and affect the economic value chain. There are a myriad of issues they could address and therefore many potential areas for a social mission. In identifying the greatest opportunity, a useful exercise is to frame each area as a sword or a shield. Where can a company go on the offensive by doing more good, and where is it more accurately described as being on the defensive by doing less bad?

DuPont, for example, the American chemicals business, could and does tackle global food security (social), reduce its carbon footprint (environmental) and improve conditions in its supply chain (economic). Improving food security could be viewed as a sword, while the others might more naturally be categorised as shields.

Most companies need to address all these issues, but "swords and shields" framing helps identify a social mission that can help drive competitive advantage, compared to actions that are required to mitigate risk and will potentially become industry norms or required by regulation. This is not to say shields are any less important than swords. They are often business critical. But you cannot build a social mission on something that stakeholders think you should be doing – or not doing – anyway.

Case study: Andrex

The "swords and shields" approach helped inform the creation of the Andrex social mission in 2014. There are lots of issues for Andrex to consider. One obvious area of interest for a company producing toilet tissue is the supply of paper and therefore the question of deforestation, a high priority for environmental campaigners. Kimberly-Clark, which manufactures Andrex, has developed a fibre sourcing policy that has been welcomed by campaigners and includes FSC (Forest Stewardship Council) certification on-pack.

Andrex also created a special range, Andrex Eco, made from 90% recycled fibre and 10% natural bamboo, based on the fact that bamboo is one of the fastest-growing plants in the world, producing significantly more fibre, on less land, than trees traditionally used to make tissue paper. This is clearly a good thing to do and helps ensure the sustainability of the business as well as the forests, but its impact on the business is more shield than sword. Environmentally friendly toilet tissue isn't driving competitive advantage in supermarket aisles.

This is also the case with Kimberly-Clark's approach to ethics in its supply chain, requiring its suppliers to respect human rights, worker safety and environmental practices. This, again, is clearly a good thing to do and should deliver positive social impact, but it's difficult to gain competitive advantage for doing what consumers would want you to do anyway if they thought about it, so this is more of a shield too.

Andrex's social mission – "to bring the dignity of improved sanitation to all" – was developed from the same brand essence that guides all its marketing and competitive positioning, including its TV advertising: namely, to "elevate the standard of clean." This mission led to a partnership with UNICEF to support sanitation programmes in Africa, retailer promotions that give the brand preferential positioning in-store, and a platform to talk about toilets and increase brand consideration. This is serving to differentiate Andrex from its competition and is very much a sword.

Matt Stone is Kimberly-Clark's UK marketing director for Family Care, which includes Andrex, and describes how the programme, now known as Toilets Change Lives,[5] has become core to the business:

> Toilets Change Lives has had one of the highest Returns on Investment (ROI) of any Andrex programme in the last two years (2018,

2019) – the highest impact on sales per pound spent, when you remove price and promotion. You only get that sort of ROI if the programme is inherent to the brand – the social mission has to connect to why your brand exists and everything else you're doing if you want to generate loyalty and returns.

This is such a seamless, intuitive thing for a brand like ours to be doing as it's in the foundations of the brand. The problem with tackling topical issues that aren't inherent to why the brand exists is that they become discretionary rather than must-have parts of the brand's activity.

The programme is now global and in some of the markets where we run it, like Brazil and South Africa, the issue of poor sanitation exists, while in others it doesn't. But because the insights underpinning it are universal, it transcends geographies and business models.

Toilets Change Lives has paved the way for more fundamental thinking about the role social missions can play in brand building, business building and making the world a better place. They have become a key part of how we think about engaging consumers and fundamental to our plans for how we win in the future.

It is often easier to find the competitive advantage of a sword in social rather than environmental or economic issues. Partly this is down to reality that, in most cases where corporates support environmental causes (like reducing their use of single-use), they are essentially committing to reducing the harm that was happening before. Compare this to social causes where they can make a new, positive difference.

But it is also down to the fact that social issues often produce an easier story to tell. Our research into Generation Z also showed that these young people found social issues more pressing "to create a better world."[6] In each of the US, UK, and Singapore surveys, young people ranked social issues (like food security, access to water and sanitation, education, and healthcare) ahead of climate change and sustainable energy as the most important issues to address. For Andrex, telling the story of the difference that having a toilet has made to a family in Angola is easier to link to its brand marketing in countries like the UK than explaining its sustainable sourcing programmes or what it is doing to promote fairness for workers in its supply chains.

This may change as the calls for action on climate change become more urgent, but the sword or shield question remains central to social mission development: is what the company is doing adding something new and better to the world, or is it reducing harmful impacts?

Identifying the social mission sword that can help drive the business forward helps answer Milton Friedman's criticism that, because a corporate executive is the agent of the shareholders and their primary responsibility is to them, then they have no business deciding how to spend their money out of some sense of social responsibility. Identifying social mission swords that drive growth in the corporation is entirely in line with Friedman's argument that "a corporate executive is an employee of the owners of the business. He has direct responsibility to his employers. That responsibility is to conduct the business in accordance with their desires, which generally will be to make as much money as possible while conforming to the basic rules of the society, both those embodied in law and those embodied in ethical custom."

In today's world – transformed through globalisation and digital transparency since Friedman's fiercely argued 1970 essay against the notion of corporate social responsibility – a social mission is, in fact, becoming an essential tool to deliver on his core belief: that "The Social Responsibility of Business is to Increase its Profits."[7]

NOTES

1 https://www.bbc.co.uk/news/uk-44413586.

2 Russell, Bertrand (1930). *The Conquest of Happiness*. New York: H. Liveright.

3 http://coffeevsgangs.telegraph.co.uk/.

4 https://www.knorr.com/uk/future50report.html.

5 https://www.kimberly-clark.com/en/responsibility/social-impact/toilets-change-lives.

6 https://mullenlowesalt.com/blog/2015/05/generationz-uk/.

7 https://www.nytimes.com/1970/09/13/archives/a-friedman-doctrine-the-social-responsibility-of-business-is-to.html.

HOW TO BUILD A SUSTAINABLE BRAND

A sustainable brand – whether a consumer brand in a supermarket aisle or a corporate brand in a business park – is one that understands its relationship with the wider world and acts on it. Living up to a social purpose tied to commercial success is what makes a brand sustainable.

When *Financial Times* (the "world's leading business publication") says it's "time to reframe capitalism"[1] and *The Economist* asks, "What are companies for?"[2] it's clear something is happening. In the midst of these calls for change the language around business and sustainability has yet to coalesce to generally agreed definitions. Talk of responsible business and social missions, corporate purpose and sustainability can serve to confuse.

But the central question that businesses and brands need to answer is: What is your purpose in the world? Why do you exist for your shareholders and staff, customers and communities, and, crucially, what would they miss – really miss – if you no longer existed?

To answer these questions today – to be a sustainable brand – brands need to find their social purpose. What is it that they do that connects their business to society; that makes them stand out with their customers, gives meaning to their employees, and delivers sustainable growth to their shareholders?

We can answer these questions by following the PURPOSE process:

1 **P**rime the brand
2 **U**ncover the issue
3 **R**eal commitment
4 **P**lan

DOI: 10.4324/9781003176817-6

5   Operationalise
6   Set in motion
7   Evaluate

1   **Prime the brand**. Brands – corporate and consumer – are multifaceted. They exist in the way they are communicated and presented to the world; in the functionality of what they do as products and services; in the behaviours of the people who manage and represent them; in their social, environmental, and economic impacts; in their reputation (what others say about them) and their heritage.

Each facet reveals an opportunity to find the brand's social mission:

Action 1: Appoint a "brand journalist" to explore the brand's heritage, interview its stakeholders and review research data. This covers why the brand came into existence in the first place, the role it plays today in people's lives and how it positions itself in the world. This ensures the process starts in the right place to find a social purpose that is uniquely ownable by that brand. It also starts the process of uncovering stories and insights that will inform communications around it.

This step also assesses business resilience. The brand journalist reviews the brand with the mind-set of an investigative journalist looking to expose hypocrisy. Does the way the organisation treats its workers inside the organisation and across its supply chain – stack up against a declaration of intent around a social issue? Do manufacturing processes or corporate policies match the promise of "doing good"? Does the company have a history of poor performance in this space?

Unearthing problems and inconsistencies doesn't necessarily mean the brand isn't ready to proceed, but it does mean that it needs to have credible shields alongside its social sword: has enough been done to address past issues? Is there credible assurance of long-term improvement? Is there a commitment to transparency?

Issues around GlaxoSmithKline's release or non-release of antiretroviral patents for HIV drugs, for example, shouldn't prevent the company from acting to address health needs in sub-Saharan Africa, but they do require credible commitments to reform.

2 **Uncover the issue**. Which social issue is right for your brand? Which issue do you have a right or obligation to address? Which can you address as a natural extension of your core business? What do your customers care about and what will engage opinion formers and arouse genuine public interest?

The Sustainable Development Goals offer one framework for identifying potentially relevant issues, as do the existing social, environmental, and economic impacts of the brand. Where the overall territory is obvious or readily agreed – Domestos or Andrex getting involved in sanitation, for example – this stage can focus on breaking down the issue into potential areas of focus within the broader territory.

Competitor activity is considered here, but the fact that a competitor may be active in an area doesn't preclude it as a social purpose territory. It does, however, clarify the question of where the brand can make a distinct difference. For example, while a number of feminine hygiene brands address girl empowerment as a social issue, Procter & Gamble's Always and Essity's Bodyform brands have been able to carve out distinctive territories with their #LikeAGirl[3] and Project V[4] programmes respectively.

Potential territories are researched and shortlisted. A review of social media engagement on the issues as well as consumer research data are important indicators for whether a brand's involvement in particular issues will "catch." Latent issues that don't show up in research can still offer opportunities for brands, especially where they are able to use their scale to bring the issue to wider public consciousness. These latent issues can often be found in the work of subject experts. Dove, for example, decided to raise the issue of self-esteem of adolescent girls before it was being widely discussed by the public, but after it was already being talked about by academics and psychologists. Interviews with experts in the territory – academics, charities, NGOs – build understanding of the real issues to be addressed and also help identify potential supporters for future campaigns.

Action 2: Convene a workshop involving all relevant stakeholders inside the business as well as external experts to assess shortlisted territories against the defining ASCEND criteria:

Alignment to the corporate strategy. Will a social purpose addressing this issue win corporate backing?

Strong link to the product or service: Would a busy customer realise instantly why you were involved in this issue without needing to have the connection explained?

Clear commercial interest: Does the issue matter in the markets that matter to your products or services and can it be helpful to your business to address it?

Encouragement to others to join: Is there genuine public interest in the issue, to make it campaignable? Are governments and NGOs already tackling it?

Narrative for the brand story: How easily does the issue fit with existing brand communications and tone of voice? Can the brand be uniquely helpful?

Drives engagement across the organisation: does the issue resonate with the workforce? Can they get involved in addressing it?

Potential territories for Nike, for example, might include gender equality, youth unemployment and obesity. The ASCEND criteria point to gender equality as an issue not only that Nike can do more to impact but also one that can be easily linked to its products and commercial interests and can help tell the brand story.

The workshop helps identify the specific role the brand can play in addressing the issue: what social good can the brand deliver and how would this contribute to brand growth to make it sustainable? It then identifies a defendable, differentiated approach to tackling the issue and initial thoughts on partners with whom the brand could work.

3 **Real commitment**. The core group now develops a commitment to action: what is the brand actually going to do to improve the situation? A partner is normally essential in delivering any social purpose. Sometimes the distribution of a brand's products or delivery of its services can bring social good in and of itself (like a toothpaste reducing tooth decay), but even then a partner will be required to endorse methodologies and provide credible impact measurements (increased tooth brushing frequency, for example).

Potential partners are reviewed according to specific expertise, area of operation and compatibility. This core group selects the partner or partners to work with and negotiates the partnership, for at least the first year. The contribution to the partnership (through finances, resources, expertise or a combination of all three) has to be equivalent to the business benefit the brand seeks. Too little and it looks like greenwashing; too much and it won't be sustainable. The group therefore also has to set out what business returns are expected, how these will be measured and be transparent about this in negotiating with partners.

Action 3. Draw up a social purpose charter committing to specific action, transparency of measurement, and clear business returns.

4   **Plan**. The core team then creates the full social purpose plan, with responsibilities allocated, goals set, partnerships agreed and communications prioritised.

Action 4. Finalise the social purpose plan with agreed business and social impact targets. A pilot programme is identified with a clear process for incorporating learnings.

5   **Operationalise**. In parallel with the Plan stage, the social purpose has to be linked to the internal systems and processes of the business, including commercial plans. This operationalising also involves making sure it is aligned with all existing sustainability commitments.

The previous development stages are designed to align key stakeholders, but the wider organisation also needs to be brought on board – corporate affairs, HR, sales, and so on. This can be done through existing internal communications channels and external media, but a "ladder of engagement" can also help drive alignment behind the social purpose. The ladder creates opportunities for employees to get involved, from low-level activities like idea sharing or clicking their support on social media platforms, to higher involvement through integration into existing work streams and volunteering.

Action 5. Draw up an employee engagement plan to ensure the social purpose is known about, understood and actively supported.

6   **Set in motion**. The social purpose is launched in a pilot market where impacts can be measured, lessons learned, and improvements made. Brand authenticity is key to the acceptance and success of a social mission inside and outside the organisation. A manifesto is created that sets out the brand's reason for

involvement in the issue and its commitment to action, alongside a message house and tone-of-voice guidelines that help everyone stay on-brand as well as on-plan.

7   **Evaluate**. Social impact and business results (including understanding and support for the social mission inside the organisation) are assessed against the key performance indicators in the plan to feed into ongoing development.

As we saw in Chapter 2, Paul Polman committed Unilever to linking business success to increased social and reduced environmental impacts. "We need business models to drive new forms of long-term capitalism – mindful, responsible and inclusive."[5]

How has Unilever translated that vision into practice inside the organisation? How have they gone about embedding purpose not only into brands like Lifebuoy, Dove, and Domestos but into the core operations model so that all of its brands can become sustainable brands, or Sustainable Living Brands in its terminology.[6]

Alan Jope replaced Paul Polman as Unilever CEO in 2019. In a new interview for the second edition of this book, he describes how the company continues to put its relationship with society and the environment at the heart of its commercial strategy.

Alan Jope

On Unilever and purpose

We're 100 years plus into this journey, but after my predecessor put purpose front and centre again, it's easy to forget that three years into having the Unilever Sustainable Living Plan at the heart of the business, there were still a lot of people in the organisation who were wondering whether it was going to stick, or assuming it was going to pass. It takes years of disciplined focus from leaders in organisations, and especially I suppose the chief executive, to make this everyone's priority.

Purpose is at the absolute heart of the company's mission to make sustainable living commonplace, and of our vision to be recognised as the world leader in sustainable business, linking all that of course to financial outcomes. Up until 2019, we had a business strategy and a sustainability strategy, which didn't seem very sensible to me, so we've brought these together. If you can't find sustainability and purpose in your strategy, that's probably a good clue that it's a bit secondary.

On embedding purpose into the business

There's a whole bunch of levers that a CEO must pull if you want purpose to really gain traction in a business. We have now enshrined purpose in our recruitment and our leadership development tools. We talk about seven characteristics of leaders at Unilever. We think about it as your inner game and your outer game. Three of the leadership characteristics relate to your inner game, how you show up, and one of these is your sense of purpose, so we hire and develop for purpose.

It's also in all of our rewards, so all 14,000 managers in Unilever are on a long-term incentive programme where 25% of it relates to our performance against purpose and environmental metrics. Given that we've been at this very publicly for over ten years now, most people in Unilever have joined in part because of our commitment in these spaces.

On responsible business and commercial success

There's been a dominant paradigm in the world, that there is trade-off between conducting your business responsibly and good financial outcomes in the short term. I profoundly reject that. I really believe that our brands will be more relevant, our customer relationships will be more rewarding, our innovation will be better, our consumption of resources – and therefore our cost profile – will go down, and that we'll be a magnet for talent, if we conduct our business responsibly.

If you do believe that paradigm, you will find it more difficult to stay focussed on your environmental and social impact when the business is under pressure. If you reject the paradigm though, you can make progress as a responsible business all the time. When the business is in flow, when we're doing well, we can think a bit longer term, we can be a bit bolder, more ambitious on our goals, push forward on some of the big things we want to do on the environment, on plastics, on carbon ... put people on fair living wages. It's easier to pull the trigger on those things when the business is doing well.

But even when we have a problem, purpose is central to our response. We've been stuck growing at 3% for four consecutive years now and for our model to work we really need to be growing at around 4%. It doesn't sound that complicated, and in trying to restore or find that extra growth we have developed what we call our five growth fundamentals. The first of these is purposeful brands, because we feel so strongly that that is how our brands remain relevant into the future.

On corporate versus brand initiatives

There are some aspects of our business where corporate scale really matters, such as the commitments that we make around carbon or sustainable sourcing, around the use of plastics or on radical transparency. Those things only work when you do them as a corporation, but then there's absolutely no point doing them as a corporation if consumers aren't able to make brand choices based on some of the things that we're proud of doing. So it's a little bit of a shock 10 years into the Unilever Sustainable Living Plan, if you grab most of our brands or look at most of the advertising and realise how few carry an overt social or environmental purpose impact in the advertising. It is very much my intent that more of our brand communication is overtly purposeful and that we talk more about what we're doing on the brands and not just at a corporate level, and we're seeing good progress on that.

We do think that we have a competitive advantage in understanding that talking the talk has to be complemented by walking the walk. That standing up and advertising your point of view on something is not as powerful as actually doing stuff. The fact that Dove has talked to 35 million girls about self-esteem; the fact that Domestos has got 18 million toilets installed; the fact that almost every brand is taking action, not just making proclamations; this is the key. We don't understand why many of our competitors haven't done that yet.

Strategy is not a matter of what you could do, but what you should do. When someone drops me a note and says, 'would you consider sponsoring our schools new minibus?', well obviously it's not a bad thing to do, but we have to focus on where we can have the most material impact. The reason why I think Volvo is associated with safety is because they didn't talk about or focus on anything else for four decades and the minute they deviated from that, they sort of lost their mojo a bit. I want Domestos, for example, to be 100% focussed on toilet hygiene. Even if there's a role they could play on something else, they should say no, that's not our focus. We want each brand to be maniacally focussed on their own purpose.

On investors and ESG

We want to be the Harvard Business School case study on how responsible business drives better financial outcomes and more and more investors are seeing that, even in the short time that I've been in this seat. Previously, we'd visit an investor and of half a dozen people, one would be the ESG person who would ask questions, often very detailed questions, about what we're doing from an ESG perspective. Now those questions are more likely to come from the portfolio managers themselves, which is a great change.

On partnerships

We're still healthily competitive but I don't think any one of our brands will be able realise their purpose without some kind of partnership. So we work with NGOs, with government bodies, with other companies. Take the plastic agenda, for example. The collection and recycling of plastic requires that horrible term, ecosystem change, and we'll need to work with bodies that represent waste pickers, with new technology companies that help us with chemical recycling, with recycling companies, resin manufactures, NGOs, just to get that whole chain working. Whether its environmental impact or social impact, the ability to partner – and the genuine desire to partner – is essential and has to be at the heart of every single brand.

Unilever's success has been built through leadership clarity, organisational alignment, and brand focus. Successive CEOs have made it clear that the success of the business depends on understanding and acting on the company's relationship with the wider world; on processes and incentives that keep the organisation driving towards that vision; and on individual brands focussing on where they can make the biggest difference socially, environmentally, and commercially.

As CEO of one of the world's biggest advertisers, Alan Jope declaring his intent that "more of our brand communication is overtly purposeful" is significant for the marketing and communications industry, as we shall see in the next chapter.

NOTES

1 https://aboutus.ft.com/press_release/ft-sets-the-agenda-with-new-brand-platform.

2 https://www.economist.com/briefing/2019/08/22/big-business-is-beginning-to-accept-broader-social-responsibilities.

3 https://always.com/en-us/about-us/our-epic-battle-like-a-girl.

4 https://www.bodyform.co.uk/our-world/project-v/.

5 https://www.huffpost.com/entry/paul-polman-why-the-role_b_7652954.

6 https://www.unilever.co.uk/news/press-releases/2020/unilever-celebrates-10-years-of-the-sustainable-living-plan.html.

7

COMMUNICATIONS AS A DRIVER OF CHANGE

Good, the more communicated, more abundant grows.[1]

John Milton, *Paradise Lost*

Marketing and communications have had a troubled relationship with how business engages with society. The term "Greenwash" was invented to describe how companies tried to cover up their true motives or deflect attention away from more controversial issues.

The practice developed as the environmental movement grew in the 1960s and newly greened corporate images started to appear. "Greenwash" itself was first described by New York environmentalist Jay Westervelt in 1986. He used it to characterise the signs we're now familiar with seeing in hotel rooms asking us to reuse towels to 'save the planet, signs that omit to mention the saving in laundry costs this makes for the hotel owners. The practice reached its low water mark on Earth Day 20 in 1990 when DuPont released a corporate ad of seals clapping, whales jumping, and flamingos flying to the soundtrack of Beethoven's "Ode to Joy." This ad, designed to project the company's new-found green image, aired shortly before DuPont was named by the Environmental Protection Agency as the largest emitter of toxic waste in the US.

This was the story of marketing's relationship to social and environmental issues. But in a more transparent age where greenwashing is called out so readily – through organisations like CorpWatch and campaigns like Greenpeace's #stopgreenwash – marketing and communications can no longer be about polishing reputations without substantive action. The days of talking the talk without walking the

DOI: 10.4324/9781003176817-7

walk – brand say without brand do – are coming to an end, as "Purposewash" has joined "Greenwash" on the no fly list.[2]

Marketing and communications, however, can play more positive roles in building trust and effecting change inside and outside businesses.

Pressure groups exist to bring about change and tend to be highly adept at using communications to accelerate that change. Greenpeace's highly sophisticated "Give orang-utans a break" assault on the Kit Kat brand in 2010[3] quickly led to parent company Nestlé announcing it would identify and remove any companies in its supply chain with links to deforestation.

Corporates too are now adopting the power of external communications as an accelerator of change, including with internal audiences. Going external with a social mission can have powerful internal results.

The public communication of a social mission helps to persuade the internal audience that a company means what it says. There's no going back once it's in the public domain, whereas employees in any organisation might remain cautious about pledges made in internal memos or meeting rooms. Suddenly they are liberated to be open about their own passions rather than worry that being enthusiastic about a social mission is somehow not the corporate thing to do or might even be career-limiting. In this way employee engagement (and improvements in productivity) can be built disproportionally quickly by the public communication of a social mission.

We've observed ten methods of communicating a social mission that encourage employee engagement. The examples come from Unilever, which, as we have seen, is recognised by GlobeScan, The Economist and others as having the best grip on "enlightened capitalism"; is seeing its growth driven by its "Sustainable Living Brands"; and recognised by LinkedIn as a "Top Attractor" and the number one FMCG company to work for globally.

Ten ways to drive positive change internally through social missions:

1   **Shout from the top**. Unless the leader of the company is seen to be an active supporter of the company's social mission, it will remain in the silo of a Corporate Affairs or Sustainability department. Paul Polman was unapologetic in his communications that

the future of capitalism lies in a more progressive relationship with society and communicated that belief on so many platforms that not one of his company's 170,000 employees could have failed to recognise that the company's social and business purpose were one and the same.

2   **A Clause IV moment.** Tony Blair famously persuaded wavering British voters in 1997 that they could safely elect a Labour government after 18 years by revising Clause IV of the party's 80-year-old constitution, a clause that committed the party to secure 'common ownership of the means of production, distribution and exchange'. The clause was celebrated and feared in equal measure and widely held to be a barrier to large sections of the population voting Labour. Blair revised the clause to remove the nationalising principles and his 'Clause IV moment' was seen as a defining moment in the transition from old to New Labour.

Although not quite as headline-grabbing as Blair's, Paul Polman gave Unilever its own Clause IV moment on his appointment as chief executive officer in 2009 when he announced, "We don't do three-month profit reporting anymore. We're not going into the three-month rat-races. We're working for the consumer, we are focused, and the shareholder gets rewarded."[4] Recalling the decision later he said, "We needed to remove the temptation to work only toward the next set of numbers. Our share price went down 6 percent when we announced the ending of guidance, as many saw this as a precursor to more bad news. But that didn't bother me too much; my stance was that in the longer term, the company's true performance would be reflected in the share price anyway."[5]

This announcement demonstrated to sceptical media, campaigning groups, and, above all, employees that the company really was serious about changing the way it did business and that capitalism had to evolve and form a longer-term, more sustainable relationship with society.

3   **Put other leaders on the record.** Just as critical to landing the message inside the company have been the public platforms taken by other leaders in the business, committing themselves and their divisions to the new approach. When country chairmen and category vice presidents started to state publicly that

their divisions were committed to a more sustainable way of doing business that saw the company's social responsibilities as opportunities, then it became clear to everyone inside those divisions that the new approach was permanent and wasn't vulnerable to changes in personnel at the top.

4   **Normalise it.** While communications are important to changing the way people inside the organisation think about their company, making sustainability and social purpose part of the everyday working of the business requires changes to systems and processes to make it part of business as usual.

In Unilever's case, their product brands were assessed through a "Brand Imprint" process to identify their social, environmental, and economic impacts, alongside the opportunities that existed with consumers, retail customers, and opinion formers. These became the building blocks for brands to find social missions. A specialist team was established, the Unilever Sustainable Living Plan (USLP) team, to help all parts of the business develop baseline measurements for their impacts (negative and positive) and create programmes that could deliver social progress and business growth together. Brand keys – the blueprint for its global brands – were redrawn to include a "USLP ambition."

5   **Involve people in the journey.** Initiatives like the Brand Imprint process involved employees from different areas of the business, from marketing and research and development to supply chain and finance. People across the business were encouraged and supported to contribute to the development of social missions in their area, and operating companies measured against targets for their employees taking part in "Bright Future" activities.

6   **Celebrate heroes**. Some parts of the business were ahead of others when it came to having a social mission. Ben & Jerry's, the ice cream business, was established by Ben Cohen and Jerry Greenfield in Burlington, Vermont, in 1978, with an overt social conscience that has been central to its business strategy and success. Unilever bought Ben & Jerry's in 2000, saying that it hoped to carry on the tradition of engaging "in these critical, global economic and social missions."[6]

In addition to brands like Ben & Jerry's being brought into the company, other brands already in the business were raising the role of social mission. Lifebuoy had rediscovered its founding principles and Dove had launched the Campaign for Real Beauty in 2004 in the area of women's empowerment. These brands were held up as paradigms of the new approach, and people who worked on the development of their social missions were lauded as heroes in the business. Both Lifebuoy and Dove appointed global directors of their social missions and in 2014 each gave a TED Talk on the subject: Myriam Sidibe of Lifebuoy (interviewed later in this book) on "The simple power of hand-washing"[7] and Meaghan Ramsey of Dove on 'Why thinking you're ugly is bad for you."[8] Making heroes of these brands and the people who worked on them encouraged other parts of the business to follow suit.

7 **Use social missions to attract and liberate young talent.** As we have seen above, our own Generation Z research showed that a significant proportion of young people about to enter the workforce (16- to 20-year-olds) rank working for a company that helps make the world a better place as important a consideration as salary (58% in Singapore, 45% in the UK, and 59% in the US).[9]

Deloitte's Millennial Survey in 2015 found that six in ten Millennials (those born since 1983) cited a sense of purpose as part of the reason they chose to work for their current employers, rising to 77% among higher users of social media. And 47% of this group believed that the purpose of business is to "improve society/protect the environment."[10] Companies seem to be listening as the 2020 survey reported that 69% of Millennials and 70% of Gen Z (born since 1995) felt that their employer had a "positive effect on communities."[11]

An explicit social mission is clearly a powerful tool not only to attract young talent into an organisation (helping to explain why Unilever started to rank alongside Google and Apple as an "in-demand" employer) but also to engage them once they are there.

8 **Earn the trust of credible third parties.** Third parties play an increasingly important role in determining a company's reputation and licence to operate as discussed in Chapter 4. They are seen to provide an objective view not only on the company's products and services and the way it conducts business but also

on what it's like to work there. When Unilever opened the doors of its supplier factories in Vietnam to Oxfam to investigate labour rights in the supply chain – resulting in a 2013 report that was critical of the company's performance in a number of areas – this sent a message not only to external stakeholders that the company was committed to transparency and improving workers' conditions but also to people inside the company that its fine words about social missions could be trusted.[12]

9   **Speak in your normal voice.** There is a temptation when companies talk about social mission for them to change the way they speak. Often this involves a descent into worthiness and hushed tones, in guilt-ridden reverence to the forces of good. Talking about a social mission differently to how the business normally talks is dangerous for two reasons. First, it often as not smacks of insincerity and does nothing to change perceptions, nothing to build trust, and nothing to stop accusations of greenwash. Second, and central to engaging employees, it sends a subliminal message to employees that this stuff isn't really part of the business.

Campaigning organisations understand instinctively the importance of tone of voice, and use the brand's own tone of voice to increase the pressure on it. Greenpeace's 2014 campaign targeting Procter & Gamble's Head and Shoulders talked about "100% rainforest destruction," mirroring the brand's own "100% flake free" claim.[13] Brands have to follow through and talk about social causes in the same voice and with the same brand personality that they use to talk about everything else. So, within Unilever, Domestos's campaigns to tackle the sanitation crisis use the same "kill germs" language as its TV ads, and Lifebuoy's social mission campaigns, like the award-winning 2013 *Gondappa* film,[14] apply the same degree of creativity as its other marketing activities.

10 **Say it's business**. Above all, the key to landing a social mission inside an organisation is to say that it's business. Unless the leadership of the company is unambiguous that they are pursuing a social mission because it makes good business sense, then not only will investors quite reasonably question why the board they are trusting with their money is spending it on things that don't grow the value of their shares (and in effect making charitable

donations on their behalf without consulting them), but the organisation won't come with them either. Individuals may commit to the social mission because they are personally motivated (like the "green crusaders" shopping at M&S, described in Chapter 5); others because their bosses tell them to. But you can never engage the organisation fully unless everyone believes it will drive the business forward, and that means being explicit that the purpose of the social mission is to drive growth.

Externally, more open communication helps build trust with NGOs, campaigners and other organisations needed to bring a social mission to life. Businesses who want to partner with NGOs are often asking their new friends to make a difficult journey, from corporate watchdog to corporate partner. This requires some leap of faith. Coupled with the fact that it also requires a change in fundraising models from grants and public donations to corporate funding, it's easy to understand why some NGOs remain wary about fully embracing these partnerships. Highly visible public declarations of intent from business leaders can give them the confidence to do so.

For external audiences, the best social mission communications follow three simple rules. They set the long-term direction, continue to tell the story of the journey along the way even when things aren't going according to plan, and are transparent as to the commercial motives.

The three rules for communicating social missions externally:

1   **Set the long-term direction**. Setting and communicating a clear direction for a social mission liberates people throughout an organisation to talk passionately and freely to external audiences (everyone from their friends and family to business partners and the media) about what the company is doing. They can be the company's best advocates. When Sir Andrew Witty at GSK said of a flagship social programme that "we are ... not looking to make a loss – we need it to be sustainable," the direction the company was travelling in was clear.[15]

2   **Tell the story of the journey.** A social mission involves tackling big, difficult, long-term issues. These are different to many of the issues businesses typically communicate about, over which they have more control. Acquisitions are generally kept quiet

until they have been completed; sales results are black and white and announced after the event; appointments and restructures are only announced once they have been finalised.

Social missions are different. It's not possible, or desirable, to wait until everything has been completed before communicating about a social mission. The best communications state the ambition, update on progress, celebrate successes and acknowledge missed targets. Missing targets isn't great, but it happens in social issues because of any number of complicating factors and externalities. It's not the same great corporate sin as missing financial targets, where shareholders have made investments based on company projections and forecasts. In the social case, missed targets will still normally mean that progress has been made and people have benefitted. Lessons have to be learned, of course, and programmes adjusted, but being open about what's not working as much as what is working plays surprisingly well with societal stakeholders and a public sceptical of business.

3   **Be transparent about the commercial motives.** Finally, transparency about the commercial motives of a programme is absolutely critical to winning trust and to the overall success of the programme. Business needs to pursue business objectives if any initiative is to be sustainable. The desire for businesses to address social issues, and the acceptance that this has to involve commercial gain, is only going to grow as the influence of Generation Z grows, as the previous research indicates.

So, if communications are such an important driver of change, what of the marketing services and advertising agencies who communicate on behalf of businesses and brands? Campaigners recognise their power and influence. In 2019, Extinction Rebellion wrote an open letter to the "Founders, CEOs, CCOs, CMOs, CFOs, MDs and CDs of the advertising industry" headed "You didn't think we'd forget about you?"[16] In it, they urged the industry to use its power to help tackle climate change.

Michael Roth is executive chairman of Interpublic Group (IPG), one of the "Big Four" marketing services groups.[17] In this interview for the second edition of this book he gave his views on the changes happening to the relationship between business and society and the role of marketing.

Michael Roth

On consumer marketing

There's always the commodity part of this where the lowest price is going to prevail. Our role in the marketing and communication business is to add something to the brand that counters the commodity aspect of the product. And if it's a brand relationship where the brand stands for something, consumers are more likely to want to do business with that company. So at least the brand is positioned in a way that it can compete with the lowest price. Now, of course, the product itself has to be ethical, and the efficacy of the work and the product have to be there, but when push comes to shove people would rather do business with a company that has the same values than not.

On employees

Employees want to work with a company that is purpose-led, and that's where, I think, we, IPG, have made great strides in terms of distinguishing ourselves from our competitor set. Early on we started with diversity and inclusion as a key component of the DNA of our company. We're leading the industry and I hear that from our clients.

In terms of making sure that our people are diverse in all ways, inclusivity isn't just about race or gender, it's people with all sorts of differences and, frankly, in order for us to communicate in the marketplace, we need those different perspectives. Our work has to reflect that and if we don't have the talent then we can't do our clients any service.

On the purpose of a company

I'm a firm believer that the stakeholders of a company aren't just the shareholders, it's society, it's the consumers, it's our vendors, it's our employees, and our actions should be able to support all of those different constituents. I was an attorney by training, so the question was, does a company have a responsibility to the shareholders just to make money, distribute it to their shareholders and let them decide where the money goes? There's all sorts of case law in terms of whether corporations are permitted to focus beyond shareholder value. And in Delaware [where over half of publicly traded US companies are incorporated], it's pretty well established that corporations do have a wider responsibility to all stakeholders, and the Business Roundtable[18] embraced that in terms of the principles which we signed on.

On the social responsibility of digital platforms

Digital now outspends traditional media, and it's growing in double digits. So we have to be able to use all those distribution outlets to get our story out and reach the consumer. The other part of it is data analytics. We have extensive data analytics capabilities as we want to make sure we're reaching the right consumer, and that we have the right tools to get that message to that consumer, and included in that message are the sustainable goals and what the company stands for, what our clients stand for.

From the outset, I've said these platforms have responsibilities, they're not just a pipe to distribute information. They have a responsibility of what goes on their platform. We're seeing it real time right now, and it's a relevant question for us in the marketing communications side of business, because we have to protect our clients' brands.

On the pressures on companies from shareholders and stakeholders to have a plan for improving ESG impacts

Oh, I think it's real. I'm experiencing it with our own investor base. But more importantly it's our employee base and our client base that has a vested interest in this. Early on we looked at this and concluded this is a business imperative; it's not just a nice thing to do. Relationships with brands depend on it, so a lot of the work that we're doing now with our clients is to sustain the brands in a way that develops that lasting relationship. And if we don't stand for values that are consistent with the consumer, they're not going to want to do business with us.

Certainly, talking to the investment community, the sense I have is that their door into this world has been risk mitigation, but it feels like now they're beginning to see it as a growth driver for business.

On the future of marketing services

Because the world is so complex, clients need help navigating ESG, navigating media, all these different parts, and what we want to do as a company is help them with solutions. And if we don't understand the risks associated with the solutions, we have no place doing that.

> If you look at the companies we've bought and added to our portfolio, it's all consistent with that because we have to have the tools and the resources to help our clients, on ESG and brand building, competing on the internet, I mean that's the number one question that these brands have is how can we compete with the generic, low-cost provider on the internet? And the way you compete on the e-commerce platform is building your brand which includes standing for value propositions, having a great product, but also doing societal good. Consumers will appreciate that and drive their dollars there.
>
> We say no to clients who aren't consistent with our values. After the NRA position that I took,[19] I got notes from all over the world from our clients and more from our employees, saying that's why I work at IPG.

In his book on John F. Kennedy and the quest for peace, To Move the World,[20] Jeffrey Sachs describes how Kennedy "marshalled the power of oratory ... to set more peaceful relations with the Soviet Union and a dramatic slowdown in the proliferation of nuclear arms." Kennedy used a series of speeches to help bring the world's two superpowers back from the brink, notably the so-called Peace Speech at the American University in Washington, DC in June 1963.

His words made a profound difference. Communications matter, in every situation – from world peace to family relationships, from public health to business. Good communications drive positive change.

Where does that leave greenwash? The hotel industry, whose less-than-transparent communications gave rise to the term, is now having to operate in a world of mass transparency thanks to the user-generated reviews on travel websites like TripAdvisor and the challenge to their business model caused by disruptors like Airbnb.

There are signs that hotels may be moving to a more transparent conversation and relationship with their customers. Starwood Hotels, for example, which includes the Sheraton, Westin, and Aloft brands, created a "Make a Green Choice" scheme where guests can choose not to have housekeeping services and in return get a meal voucher or loyalty points. Perhaps the days of greenwash are coming to an end.

NOTES

1 Milton, John (1805). *Paradise Lost*. Gotha: Steudel.

2 https://www.campaignlive.co.uk/article/purpose-washing-damaging-industry/1456451.

3 http://edition.cnn.com/2010/WORLD/asiapcf/03/19/indonesia.rainforests.orangutan.nestle/index.html.

4 https://www.reuters.com/article/uk-sustainbility-unilever-ceo-idUK-BRE8A11FJ20121102.

5 https://www.theguardian.com/sustainable-business/unilver-ceo-paul-polman-purpose-profits.

6 United Press International (12 April 2000). Unilever buys Ben & Jerry's. http://www.upi.com/Archives/2000/04/12/Unilever-buys-Ben-Jerrys/2054955512000.

7 https://www.ted.com/talks/myriam_sidibe_the_simple_power_of_hand_washing?language=en.

8 https://www.youtube.com/watch?v=kq8VdC-3bvg.

9 https://mullenlowesalt.com/blog/2015/05/generationz-uk/.

10 https://www2.deloitte.com/content/dam/Deloitte/global/Documents/About-Deloitte/gx-wef-2015-millennial-survey-executivesummary.pdf.

11 https://www2.deloitte.com/content/dam/Deloitte/global/Documents/About-Deloitte/deloitte-2020-millennial-survey.pdf.

12 Wilshaw, Rachel, with Liesbeth Unger, Do Quynh Chi and Pham Thu Thuy (January 2013). *Labour Rights in Unilever's Supply Chain: From Compliance towards Good Practice*. Oxfam. https://www.unilever.com/Images/rr-unilever-supply-chain-labour-rights-vietnam-310113-en_tcm244-409769_ en.pdf.

13 Greenpeace (26 February 2014). Procter & Gamble brings rainforest destruction into bathrooms. Press release. http://www.greenpeace.org/international/en/press/releases/2014/ProcterGamble-brings-rainforest-destruction-into-bathrooms.

14 Unilever (5 June 2014). New Lifebuoy film tells of love and loss. https://www.unilever.com/brands/brand-stories/new-lifebuoy-film-tells-of-love-and-loss.html.

15 BBC (10 May 2013). GlaxoSmithKline launches Africa charity partnership. http://www.bbc.co.uk/news/business-22476556.

16 https://www.theguardian.com/environment/2019/may/19/extinction-rebellion-urges-ad-industry-to-use-its-power-for-good.

17 IPG owns a number of global networks and specialist agencies, and acquired salt, now MullenLowe salt, in 2017 https://www.interpublic.com/.

18 On 19 August 2019, The Business Roundtable, an association of CEOs of leading US companies, updated its Statement on the Purpose of a Corporation to read, 'companies should serve not only their shareholders but also deliver value to their customers, invest in employees, deal fairly with suppliers and support the communities in which they operate. The statement was signed by nearly 200 chief executive officers from major US corporations, including Michael Roth. https://www.nytimes.com/2019/08/19/business/business-roundtable-ceos-corporations.html.

19 https://www.campaignlive.co.uk/article/interpublic-declines-nra-pitch/1588610.

20 Sachs, Jeffrey (2013). *To Move the World: JFK's Quest for Peace*. New York: Random House.

8

STRANGE BEDFELLOWS

When the *Financial Times* first reported on Lifebuoy's handwashing programmes in Kibera, it described a novel feature of the work as the corporation having gained "unlikely bedfellows: UNICEF, USAID, the London School of Hygiene and Tropical Medicine, the Bill and Melinda Gates Foundation, and several non-governmental organisations."[1] It was echoing a phrase the newspaper had used in 2005 in an article headlined *Globalisation's strange bedfellows* on Unilever opening its operations in Indonesia to Oxfam to analyse the multinational's socio-economic impact there.[2]

What may have seemed unlikely bedfellows then are becoming the norm now. Businesses, governments, and NGOs – the private, public, and third sectors – are getting more and more used to working together, and any business that wants to engage in a more productive and sustainable relationship with society has to form partnerships at some point with the NGOs and other organisations that exist to champion social and environmental causes and bring about positive change.

NGOs typically offer corporates three things in partnerships: credibility, expertise, and reach. Credibility extends from using a logo on-pack or a spokesperson in PR, to support in accessing government, academic and even funding support. The Rainforest Alliance logo on packets of tea says we can take more than the tea company's word for it that the tea is sourced ethically and sustainably. Equally, WaterAid lobbying the UN and national governments to give greater prominence and support to sanitation programmes adds huge credibility to the commercial voices of the toilet bleach, tissue, and pan manufacturers.

DOI: 10.4324/9781003176817-8

Second, the expertise of NGOs in their particular field is critical to corporate partners who are often entering uncharted waters. They may have their own related expertise – which brings its own value to the partnership – but typically they don't have the institutional knowledge and know-how that exists in the dedicated NGO. Domestos might understand killing germs and people's attitudes to toilets, but UNICEF has deep-rooted expertise in improving sanitation in the developing world.

Third, the NGO will likely be better positioned to reach the beneficiaries of social mission programmes. Sometimes this overlaps with a business's own networks. Lifebuoy and UNICEF are a good example of this. UNICEF's WASH (Water, Sanitation, and Hygiene) programmes target communities who suffer the consequences of not having access to these basic requirements for life, including the poorest of the poor. Lifebuoy targets consumers who buy soap. Some of these are low-income consumers who overlap with UNICEF's targets. Others are in higher-income groups. UNICEF doesn't target the higher-income groups, Lifebuoy doesn't target the poorest of the poor. But in the middle is an overlapping group where the two organisations can work together towards common aims.

Thus, NGOs can bring corporates credibility, expertise, and reach. In return, corporate partners can bring a range of benefits to NGOs. The most obvious is resources. The pilot Andrex promotion in-store generated £250,000 for UNICEF's work in Angola, for example. Another is awareness. Stand-out films from brands like Nike, Always, and Dove generate greater awareness for gender equality through broadcast and social media than any NGO could hope to achieve alone. And corporates bring new expertise to their NGO partners, too.

When ManpowerGroup works with partners like Junior Achievement or with governments on youth unemployment programmes, it is able to transfer its expertise in how to help people become work-ready. The company's everyday business skills enable their partners to have greater impact.

Marc Van Ameringen was the executive director of GAIN – the Global Alliance for Improved Nutrition – from 2005 to 2016. He previously worked with the Canadian Government on transition programmes in Southern Africa and in particular the political transition in South Africa with the Mandela government. GAIN was one of the first NGOs to embrace the idea of engaging with the private sector to develop different types of partnerships in the area of nutrition and food security. For this book, he talked about what makes partnerships between NGOs and the private sector work, what the future holds for them and about what each side brings to such partnerships.

Marc Van Ameringen

There is a lot more opportunity for partnerships in the sustainable development agenda and it's good that partnership has become a buzzword. There's been a big shift from partnerships just being something that the chairman's discretionary fund gives to, to something that is incorporated into the core business.

A lot of things need to happen to make a partnership work well. First, the motivation has to be clear on all sides. One of the big challenges is that often you have NGOs going into partnerships looking for money and companies looking for reputational benefit. But you quickly get into a situation where the work involved to make the partnership function goes beyond the value of reputational benefit to the company or money to the NGO.

The motivation therefore needs to be very clear and aligned at the outset, beyond just money or reputation. Partnerships work when they're well focussed on a clear deliverable. The more general the partnership is, the less well it works.

Good partners make the effort to understand where the different sides of the partnerships are coming from, because what drives them can be very different. Often you see the company side of the partnership sitting with the marketing or communications team, and they're dealing with programmatic people on the not-for-profit side. It can all be very friendly, but they're coming from very different spaces and look at the partnership differently, so they have to make the effort to understand the other's perspective. Equally, it's really important how the public face of the partnership is managed. Who takes credit and who takes the blame if things go wrong?

How the partnership deals with the question of exclusivity is important, too. If one company has the same type of partnership with five different NGOs doing the same thing, it can cause problems. You don't necessarily need to be exclusive, but the partnership has to feel important on both sides and both partners have to have skin in the game to make it work, because of the high transaction cost.

The rules of the game – how partnerships deal with conflicts of interest, disputes, reputational issues – are really important, yet are often not clearly defined at the beginning, which can lead to difficulties. How you deal with unforeseen circumstances that often have nothing to do with the partnership, but are reputationally problematic, is extremely important.

The more successful partnerships are those that are taken on by the whole institution on both sides, not just the individuals involved. Partnerships often flounder when the individuals who led them change. So in very personality-driven partnerships – which is quite typical in the US – you have to make sure that the institutions are behind them in a big way.

And the ones that work have a clear sense from the outset of what impact looks like at the end, of what resources will be required, and have an exit plan built in. But this has to be combined with an ability to adapt as political and social environments change and new people come in.

NGOs bring corporates a different type of credibility and objectivity when they form partnerships with them. They bring access to networks that are often not available to the private sector: networks in civil society, existing relations with government, relations with the scientific community, links to grassroots, community-based organisations, and all the way down to direct access to the beneficiaries of programmes.

They bring sector knowledge, both in technical areas and in business models for dealing with social goods, and resources too. Many of the partnerships that GAIN has engaged in have brought money to the table as well as technical expertise.

Corporates bring a lot of the same things to their NGO partners: access to distribution systems and supply chains; access to resources, whether that's money, people, or expertise; and the sort of knowledge and IT systems that exist in the private sector. They can also bring credibility, depending on the reputation of the company and the community the partnership is looking at, and the convening power to attract other partners.

Companies are not usually very clear about the commercial benefits they want to accrue from the partnership. Those that I've been involved in tend to look more to the reputational benefit and, longer term, you can see the link between the two. But from the not-for-profit side, this is where clarity on what success looks like is helpful. It would be helpful for companies to be more explicit about the commercial interest, but it requires a very nuanced understanding from both sides. For example, imagine a situation where the company in a partnership wants to pro- vide a branded product for free to the partnership's beneficiaries. To the company it feels like they are being helpful by supplying something for free, yet to the NGO it may feel like they're compromising their objec- tivity and promoting a particular product. Both sides need to be up-front about their motivations and concerns.

On the broader sustainable development agenda, it's quite positive what's happening, and many corporate sustainability plans have been way out ahead and will meet a lot of the SDG targets before govern- ment or other parts of society do. At a partnership level, though, it's difficult to generalise about what the future will hold because it will be different sector by sector.

Where you get away from some of the red-hot issues like GMOs or palm oil and towards some of the things that are more consensual, we are seeing a lot of real movement. In areas like agriculture, education, water, and hygiene I can point to where there's been huge movement, where people really see a value in partnerships, as an opportunity to reach more people.

In sectors like nutrition it's a lot more nuanced. I probably myself have done more than anyone to focus on partnerships with the private sector in nutrition, and I think, yes, maybe we have made some prog- ress. The biggest impact we have made through partnerships has been around fortifying staple foods across the world with micronutrients. It's part of re-engineering the food systems in countries so that everybody can get the basic vitamins and minerals that they don't get otherwise. That's involved the private sector in a big way.

But the whole nutrition sector has been handicapped by the issues around the marketing of breast milk substitutes. Most of the UN and other international organisations can't work with the top 20 food compa- nies who produce breast milk substitutes because they all violate the code on marketing it. So for partnerships in nutrition that's been a real obstacle.

It's difficult for NGOs to work with companies that might involve a reputational risk to them. NGOs – just like companies – are looking at how consumers see their brand and who can really enhance it as a part- ner. If UNICEF, for example, is considering a partnership, they take a long hard look and sometimes they have felt the connection has such a negative effect that they have dropped it.

Ultimately, from the not-for-profit side, my goal is to try and get the private sector to deliver public good as much as possible; and, if they make profit in doing that, that's all the better because it means that they'll stay in the game.

If you want to reach the poorest two billion, governments aren't going to do it, so we need the private sector, but there has to be a business model that will work for them. If there isn't some significant return on investment, you're going to lose the interest of the company and you have no other way of reaching those people. There are more people who get it than ever before, but there is opportunity to do much, much more. Right now, probably only 5%–10% of the opportunities have been tapped in terms of using markets more effectively. In the next 15–20 years, there'll be a lot more change in this space. And I can see governments using more regulatory tools to drive companies in this direction, too.

At the moment, European companies have got much a bigger social vision than North American ones. Every partnership that I've done with the US has always started with the question: who's going to pay for it? Whereas with the European ones, many of them have embraced this idea of the social mission. And the Dutch, I think, are at the top of the food chain. They're still looking to make real money, but they understand that making a better world for everybody is also good for business.

Behaviour change is critical to the work of many governments and NGOs, especially in the field of public health – to encourage everything from the take-up of malaria nets and healthier hygiene and sanitation practices, to HIV testing and safer driving. Behaviour change has been front and centre in the global response to the Covid-19 pandemic – how to persuade populations to adopt new habits like mask wearing and social distancing, and practise old ones like handwashing.

Many corporates have deep institutional knowledge in behaviour change, especially FMCG companies whose brands have to compete daily to persuade consumers to change habits or switch brands. These companies can bring their NGO partners research, understanding and methodologies for changing behaviours.

The golden rule for partnerships between these "unlikely bedfellows" is for each to recognise the contribution of the other, to acknowledge their differences, identify their shared goals, and commit to a joint plan of action. This is the key to the Lifebuoy and

UNICEF example above – to recognise where they can come together, and accept where they may be targeting different groups.

Good communication is critical to this. Because the Financial Times was right: these are unlikely bedfellows. Their stated objectives aren't the same; the cultures inside the organisations are markedly different; people in NGOs often work in the same field all their careers, whereas the norm in business is for people to move around and gain broader experience. External pressures may be forcing them closer together, like the expectations on business to engage more proactively with society and the funding difficulties for many NGOs. And SDG 17 is explicitly focussed on encouraging such collaboration.[3] But the risk of dysfunctional partnerships remains very real.

Following certain principles can help prevent this from happening.

Six principles for more effective partnerships:

1 **Be clear from the start about the mutual objective of the partnership**. This can be broad at first to build consensus but then, as the partnership matures, more specific objectives can emerge. In the Lifebuoy and UNICEF example, the broad shared objective is more people washing their hands with soap at the right moments.

2 **Be open to each partner's additional individual objectives** (for UNICEF to fight for children's rights, for example; for Lifebuoy, to build market share). Being non-judgemental about each helps build a more productive partnership.

3 **Give an equal voice at the table**. Even when partners are of very different sizes with access to different levels of resources, an equal voice leads to mutual respect. So, while two partners may not have equality of size, they can have equality of say in the partnership.

4 **Acknowledge different timescales**. Businesses – especially retail and FMCG – move very fast, whereas NGOs are often more considered and need to build more stakeholder consensus for decisions. It can take a long time to build consensus, but it is essential for any programme.

5 **Prioritise internal communications**. It is vital that both organisations recognise the benefits of the partnership and understand its objectives, and good, early internal communications can

buy time and build support for the teams responsible for the partnership to make it work. Communicating small wins can be helpful in this respect.

6   **Measure broader outcomes as well as specific outputs.** If a partnership leads to government programmes working more effectively, or to a business contributing more vigorously or systematically to sustainable development, or to a community-based organisation having a much larger-scale impact, then these outcomes may be more substantial than the itemised outputs of the partnership.

UNICEF and Lifebuoy brought the lessons they had learned from the formation of their partnership to life at the African Conference on Sanitation and Hygiene (AfricaSan) in Durban in 2008.[4] Their joint session was titled "Strange bedfellows: confessions from public–private sector collaboration." Lifebuoy was represented at that meeting by Myriam Sidibe, who was Lifebuoy's Social Mission Manager at the time. She joined Unilever in 2006 having worked in development for the International Rescue Committee in Burundi. She is also an honorary assistant professor at the London School of Hygiene and Tropical Medicine, a trustee of WaterAid, and, uniquely, has a doctorate in handwashing. In an interview for this book when she was Unilever's social mission director for Africa, Myriam talked about her experience of coming into the private sector and developing partnerships with the public sector and NGOs.

Myriam Sidibe

What attracted me to Unilever in the first place was the idea that, if you could do some good in the private sector, that would give you more scale than anything else. And this ability to get to scale is what drives me still, knowing that with every little product you can make a change to somebody. You'll never be able to get that scale anywhere else.

Yet, despite the fact that everybody's talking about public-private partnerships and getting lots of good PR, I don't think that there are very many truly successful partnerships so far, ones that put transparency at the core of what they're about and really make sure that everybody's getting something out of it, especially of course that it is really benefiting the poor.

This is where we need to stop and think. Partnerships shouldn't be about doing one-off programmes in, say, 10 villages or 1,000 people or even 100,000 people when the possibility exists for you to benefit millions or hundreds of millions. Where partnerships are lacking is very simple: the win-win-win. The win for the private sector, win for the public sector and win for the vulnerable population.

Partnerships don't work when this win-win-win is not respected right from the start. I'm not sure that people in the private sector are being brave enough in standing up to potential partners and saying, 'You don't need to partner with me if you don't want to, but I'm going to continue selling those products and I'm going to try to make them as affordable as possible because I want more and more people to wash their hands with soap because it's going to make a difference for society, and importantly because I'm going to sell more soap.'

Because, if we don't talk about brands and the need for business growth from the outset, then we have no business continuing the conversation. I think the private sector needs to be brave enough to say that, but too often we hide behind an army of people whose job it is to consider and look at the corporate reputation. Which is very important, and I understand that, but the corporate reputation can also be damaged if the win-win-win principle is not embedded by each one of its brands when they form partnerships.

It's easier of course for the private sector to approach a partnership with a pot of money, but you immediately position yourself as a sponsor then, which means both sides are assuming that the people who are sitting in the public sector can do more good than the private sector. And I'm not sure that this is the right starting point. I'm not saying that they're not doing good, but I'm just saying that that's not a partnership: it's a sponsorship, and we should be clear about it.

For an effective partnership, the conversation has to be about wanting to help some of the poorest people, but equally wanting to make sure that the business is growing. That needs to be the starting point for the private sector. The public sector needs to come to the table and say, 'I want to reach the poorest people in the villages and reduce mortality and morbidity there, so I need to do handwashing with soap there.' And then we sit down and look at the mechanisms, the techniques that exist and the products. Shying away from the product and the brand is wrong: the product is the main driver of behaviour. So, unless we have a conversation that talks about affordability, types of products, formats and marketing right at the beginning, we are setting these partnerships up to fail.

The public sector taking the moral high ground in partnership discussions is not productive and doesn't get the best of the private sector focussed on a public health objective. No self-respecting marketer is going to spend his or her time trying to do generic campaigns. To sell what? The reason why people want to buy soap is because of the smell of the soap, because of the size of the soap; it's because of the colour of the soap, because of the affordability of the soap. It's all about the brand. And that's the detail and marketing expertise that have been put into the product by the private sector.

Which is why I start every single conversation on partnership by saying I've got a PhD in public health from the London School of Hygiene and Tropical Medicine and I'm probably more qualified than anybody else here including your minister, and I have chosen to tackle public health by selling soap. Not because I want my kids to go to a great school but because it's the right thing to do in terms of access to better health and that's what I want to do.

Transparency of communication unlocks progress. I'm not asking NGOs and the UN to become our brand promoters and to go sell our products: that's not what I'm saying. It's to rethink the model that drives real sustainability and to ask what sustainability means for both the private and public sector. And then you sit down and create partnerships that work.

When I think back about my journey with Lifebuoy, the first thing I think about is how driving a social mission has been crucial to the brand's growth. And the good that you originate from a brand's growth really needs to be tied into a journey. This is what social mission as a terminology itself really captures. It captures the journey that a brand has to take to be able to create the impact that you need.

The Lifebuoy journey started when the brand itself was created with a life-saving function in mind, and its DNA was always about saving lives and wanting to make a difference. But every now and again the brand forgets what its real cause in society is. I think my role, which is very much tied into the journey of at least the last ten years in Lifebuoy, is exactly that: to be a guardian for that DNA.

I would actually divide the journey into several steps. The first step is the creation of a vision. What could be the social mission for a particular brand to address? In Lifebuoy's case, reducing child mortality and morbidity and really making a difference in Asia and Africa in terms of public health. We captured that vision as helping children reach their fifth birthday.

Then we had to translate this vision into tangible strategies to help children reach the age of five in a way that drives some sort of gain for the brand. For us, these are the consumer behaviour change programmes, the programmes that create the habit of handwashing with soap and help eliminate the cause of many children not reaching their fifth birthday.

The second element is advocacy and the creation of a global handwashing movement. We need to be seen as a leader for this cause, driving it forward. Which leads to the third element: thinking about what type of partnership would be needed to achieve this global movement.

And, finally, we needed a clinical trial – a randomised control trial – to show the difference Lifebuoy is making with its behaviour change campaign.

These have been the pillars of our social mission with Lifebuoy: consumer behaviour change, advocacy, partnerships, and evidence-based measurement.

Lifebuoy's social mission programmes and communications have now helped over a billion people develop better handwashing habits.[5] Myriam went on to become a senior fellow at the Mossavar-Rahmani Center for Business and Government at Harvard University, teaching how commercial brands can drive public health outcomes through mass behavioural change, and since the publication of the first edition of this book she has taken her learnings and beliefs into founding Brands on a Mission,[6] a movement to encourage investment in sustainable business models that address health and well-being, based on the belief that business and public health goals can align.

We have also seen the prevalence and importance of this approach grow over the last five years in our own work with partnerships like the Toilet Board Coalition,[7] Parental Leave Corporate Taskforce,[8] Real Play Coalition[9] and Transform,[10] involving organisations as varied as Facebook, IKEA, LEGO, National Geographic, the UK Government, and the World Bank.

Partnerships have also been a key feature of the response to Covid-19, not least in the public-private response to the development and deployment of vaccines, as we shall see in the next chapter.

NOTES

1 Jopson, B (15 November 2007). Unilever looks to clean up in Africa. *Financial Times*. http://www.ft.com/cms/s/0/47b3586c-931f-11dc-ad39-0000779fd2ac.html.

2 *Financial Times* (7 December 2005). Globalisation's strange bedfellows. https://www.ft.com/content/4c4b47c8-6747-11da-a650-0000779e2340.

3 https://sdgs.un.org/goals/goal17.

4 https://www.wsp.org/featuresevents/features/africasan-elevates-sanitation-and-hygiene-goals-africa.

5 https://www.unilever.com/planet-and-society/health-and-wellbeing/handwashing-for-life/.

6 https://brandsonamission.com/.

7 https://www.toiletboard.org/.

8 https://www.leavefordads.com/.

9 https://www.realplaycoalition.com/.

10 https://www.transform.global/.

THE YEAR EVERYTHING CHANGED

It can feel like the pandemic has reinvented everything – the way we work, the role of government in our lives, what community means, and what's actually important to us. But in reality, these are accelerations of existing trends rather than changes in direction. Virtual working, for example, has been on the increase for years, albeit steadily. In 2017, 43% of Americans in work said that they did at least some of that work remotely.[1] But now that lockdowns have forced office workers to get intimate with Zoom and Teams, the change is taking root in culture and accelerating from early adopters to the majority.

Early adopters had also been prioritising well-being and slowing down for some time. The Slow Movement began with a protest against the opening of a fast-food restaurant in Rome in 1986, and has been taken on by organisations like The World Institute for Slowness,[2] with its motto that "The fastest way to a good life is to slow down," and in books like *In Praise of Slow* by Carl Honoré, in which he argues for "Doing everything as well as possible, instead of as fast as possible. It's about quality over quantity in everything from work to food to parenting."[3] This trend too has sped up, ironically enough, during the pandemic pause.

The same is true of the relationship between business and society. Covid-19 has forced companies to demonstrate what they actually do to contribute to society. The "Did they help?" website[4] enables anyone to find out at a click what companies (and celebrities) did to help out during the pandemic. This site has now extended its remit to cover what companies have done in relation to the Black Lives

DOI: 10.4324/9781003176817-9

Matter movement and LGBTQ issues. Companies are being held to account for what they say and how it may differ from what they do.

This too is an acceleration of what was already happening. Before the virus took hold, investors were already piling the pressure on finance directors to show how their companies were managing their externalities in relation to the Environment and Society, the E and the S of ESG.[5] In other words, investors were already seeing that it was a risk for businesses not to understand their relationship with society or their impact on the planet.

Likewise, customers were already forcing sales directors to demonstrate their environmental and social credentials if they wanted to pre-qualify for tenders or secure the best listings in-store. Gen Z were already making it clear to marketing directors that they wanted brands to be doing stuff that matters, rather than talking empty words.[6] And activists were already driving operations and supply chain directors to clean up their factories and offices and ensure fairness in the way they source raw materials.[7]

Frank Cooper, in his interview for this book, also spoke to these trends and their acceleration during the pandemic:

> What's interesting to me is that Covid-19 has forced companies to stand up and show how they can contribute to society. Sometimes it's not even their core business, but they're using their corporations to make it happen. For example, if you look at LVMH saying you know we're pretty good at making non-consumable liquids through a formula, maybe we can make hand sanitisers. And Disney saying we know people are going to be at home, so we'll give you early access to Frozen 2 at home for free, I think it's accelerating this notion that businesses have to have some consciousness about the impact that they can have on societies.
>
> It will be fascinating to see how long the memories are in terms of who stepped up and who didn't. There are so many things you can do and there's a humanitarian element to it. I would never want to discourage anyone from doing anything on the humanitarian side. There are some companies who could donate money to food banks, but what might be more important at this point is for them to convert their production line for personal protective equipment. There are some companies that inherently say

we care about small businesses, well here's your chance to step up and show how you care about small businesses. So I think the more you can be in line with who you are, or what you do, or what your purpose is as a company, it benefits society today, but also it will benefit the brand coming out of it.

Investors are looking at who will emerge from this crisis stronger. Whenever you have a crisis there are sectors, there are companies that emerge stronger. There's a story arc to every crisis where it starts off with complete disorientation, then moves to a stabilisation period where you still don't know when the end is near, but you're looking for businesses to help stabilise your situation and your environment, and then to the light at the end of the tunnel where people are starting to think about how to emerge from it. I think investors will shift quickly to thinking about which companies will emerge from this in the strongest way, and the companies that will emerge strongest are the ones that follow their purpose and apply it to the current circumstances.

What the pandemic and our response to it as individuals, communities, businesses, nations, and the world has shown us with crystal clarity is that none of us – no person, no company, no government – can function independently and that our planet has clear and finite limits. Society exists and companies now, more than ever, need to be able to demonstrate how they contribute to it across every aspect of their business.

How will the accelerations of Covid-19, and the year that changed everything, affect how businesses operate? As Frank Cooper says, the strongest companies – the ones that will be most attractive to investors post-pandemic – are those that follow their purpose. So, what will "following their purpose" look like in the post-pandemic world?

1   **The war for talent will be increasingly fought on the purpose battlefield**. The forced realisation that most office-based jobs don't need to be based in the office means that businesses will need to find something other than physical location to bind employees to their company and find the increased productivity that an engaged workforce generates. This accelerates the need for companies to answer the "Why" with a genuine,

meaningful purpose, or risk becoming irrelevant to the talent they depend on to compete.

2   **Digital transactions transforming for good.** The acceleration of online purchasing during lockdowns was a lifeline to many businesses who could no longer interact with customers in person. But the ethics of online – from process to product – were drawn into the spotlight as consumers looked local and counted the social and human cost. Once-transactional experiences now bear a heavy weight in managing expectations and communicating ethical standards as we wake up to the impact of one-click ordering. The scrutiny we're now applying to today's purchases looks set to last long beyond the lockdown experience, changing not only channel preferences, but consideration models too across even the most commoditised of sectors.

3   **The rising power of Gen Z.** The next generation stepped up to the plate during Covid-19,[8] showing us how to stay connected and optimistic during a time of isolation from friends which might have been predicted to be more difficult for people of their age. Their preference for the unvarnished vulnerability of TikTok over the curated perfection of Instagram points to a generation who won't respond well to fake platitudes from brands. Their power and influence are accelerating, both directly through the brands they chose and indirectly through their advocacy.

This generation's coming of age has witnessed the rise of "cancel culture," a phenomenon first observed in 2016 on social media, when disappointment and anger were aimed at those deemed to have transgressed society's expectations. Cancel culture grew during the pandemic, with 74% of people in the US, for example, saying they felt more empowered than ever before to share their thoughts or opinions about companies; 64% saying that social media has given them a voice to influence companies; and 66% saying that even if they love a company's products or services, they would still cancel that company if it does something wrong or offensive. Importantly for the question, "What does follow your purpose mean?" 73% said they were less likely to cancel a company if it purpose-driven.[9]

4   **Post-pandemic partnerships.** We saw in Chapter 8 that partnerships between businesses and governments and NGOs are

critical to demonstrating genuine action and driving positive impact on societal and environmental issues. Again, this approach has been accelerated by the pandemic and post-Corona we will see the question shift from "why should we work in partnership" to "why wouldn't we." Every country's response has seen a coalition of public and private sector, local and national organisation, community and individual effort. Social and environmental problems require multi-faceted responses, and as the expectation on companies accelerates to demonstrate their social and environmental credentials, so will the expectation to follow the Covid-19 approach of working in partnership. This cuts both ways: businesses must look imaginatively for "unusual bedfellows" and be empathetic to their needs, but not-for-profit partners must also learn to be more agile and progressive in how they work with commercial partners.

5   **An increasingly social licence to operate.** Many companies have had to respond to activist and consumer-led pressures to preserve their licence to operate, recognising that the threat to their reputation is a risk that has to be managed. Beyond these pressures, the increased role of government at all levels in responding to the pandemic will accelerate the likelihood of regulation to back up public pressure and reinforce the need for businesses to deliver on their environmental and societal obligations to maintain their licence to operate. Regulating businesses may not be the first steps of government post-lockdown, but action, when it comes, is likely to be more dramatic from emboldened regulators.

History gives us some lessons as to which businesses emerge and succeed in times of great change – the narrative arc that Frank Cooper describes. The first industrial revolution gave birth to companies in Victorian England with a social mission at their heart, famous brands and businesses that endure today, like Cadbury's, Boots, and Lever Brothers.

The second industrial revolution translated into the Golden Age of management in the US, built on the Puritan belief that subordinated the interests of the individual to the group, the same belief that drove the Pilgrims on their journey towards the new world. And those principles – taken to Japan in the aftermath of the Second

World War – helped create the ingredients for the third industrial revolution, the electronics boom in the second half of the 20th century.

These purposeful principles formed the strong foundation on which successful businesses emerged from periods of turbulence.

The world will return to normal when Covid-19 passes, but it will be a gradual return, and one to a new normal in which previously gradual changes in the world have accelerated to become the new norms. Businesses everywhere will have to acknowledge that business serves society, not the other way round. And the businesses and brands that emerge strongest and best placed to succeed in a post-Covid world will be the ones who took this opportunity – this pause for many of them from the day-to-day busyness of activity – to develop strategies that don't just align their operations to this new world but also lead with this more purposeful approach to the fore.

NOTES

1 https://hbr.org/2019/08/is-it-time-to-let-employees-work-from-anywhere.

2 https://www.theworldinstituteofslowness.com/.

3 https://www.carlhonore.com/book/in-praise-of-slowness/.

4 https://didtheyhelp.com/.

5 https://mullenlowesalt.com/blog/2019/08/follow-the-money-why-brands-with-a-conscience-are-winning-on-wall-street/.

6 https://www.marketingdive.com/news/study-gen-z-cares-about-issues-and-is-skeptical-of-brands/555782/.

7 https://www.ft.com/content/3af1db14-5509-11e8-b24e-cad6aa67e23e.

8 https://www.voguebusiness.com/consumers/marketing-to-gen-z-during-covid-19.

9 https://www.porternovelli.com/findings/the-2021-porter-novelli-the-business-of-cancel-culture-study/.

10

THE FUTURE

Lifebuoy soap was born near Liverpool, in England, and is owned by an Anglo-Dutch company. As such, it is part of a northern European tradition that has often found the link between business and society more natural than other parts of the world have. This includes companies founded in Victorian England – Cadbury's, Boots, Lever Brothers – which had a social mission at their heart. Or companies like Carlsberg in Denmark and IKEA in Sweden, founded by Ingvar Kamprad in 1943 "to create a better everyday life for the many people."[1]

Different traditions in other parts of the world are pushing businesses towards the creation of sustainable brands with social missions from different starting points.

In India, where it was once said more people knew the Lifebuoy jingle than the national anthem, the sense of obligation on successful businesspeople to give back to their community is strong and was reflected in the introduction in 2014 of government guidelines requiring companies to spend 2% of their net profit on social development,[2] whereas developments in this area in China are more likely to be influenced in the long term by the Confucian tradition and sense of collectivism.

In the US, the practice of philanthropy is so embedded, and the obligations on successful business leaders to be seen to be giving back so strong, that it can feel more difficult to equate community obligations with business success. Much of this comes from the original European settlers who dealt with the seemingly conflicting pulls of their deeply held religious beliefs and their hunger to make their

DOI: 10.4324/9781003176817-10

fortunes in the new world, by working hard six days a week and giving money to the church on the seventh.

We see echoes of this today in the approach of people like Bill Gates who spent the first half of his working life making his fortune through Microsoft and is intent on spending the second half giving it away through the Gates Foundation. And in Mark Zuckerberg's announcement that he and his wife, Priscilla Chan, would give 99% of their Facebook shares "during our lives" to charitable purposes.[3]

As Jonas Prising of Manpower Group said, however, the American people are deeply pragmatic, and the business community will soon enough embrace the concept of sustainable brands with social missions if they see that they drive commercial success.

In Latin America, the desire to avoid the commercial chaos of social unrest pushes businesses towards a more proactive role in society. Businesses needs stability and have to engage in social issues if they are to enjoy conditions for growth. Take the issue of water, for example. Businesses in São Paulo are forced to invest in sourcing their own water during periods of drought where the public infrastructure cannot deliver it and deforestation in the Amazon is leading to reduced rainfall,[4] leading to conflict with local populations.

In the case of water, it is not just the crisis point of droughts that hits business and society alike and, in the worst cases, sees them competing for resources. General water stress reduces the demand for consumer goods, for example. As water becomes scarcer or more expensive, the demand for shampoos and soaps, laundry powders and dishwashing liquids goes down.

On the positive side, Natura, Brazil's largest cosmetics company, has grown by promoting itself as a sustainable brand, both through its environmental credentials and use of natural products but also through its promise of equitable sharing of benefits along the supply chain.

All over the world forces – many of them accelerated by the Covid-19 pandemic – are at play driving business towards a more sustainable relationship with society. Driving them to build sustainable brands.

Some of these businesses are also beginning to explore their very nature as companies and the way they are incorporated. The B-Corp movement started in the US in 2006 as an accreditation scheme for companies who can demonstrate their social and environmental credentials.[5] B-Corps include well-known companies like Ben & Jerry's, Patagonia, and Danone.

Natura became the world's largest publicly listed company to achieve B-Corp status in 2014. After acquiring The Body Shop in 2017, that too became a B-Corp in 2019, and following its acquisition of Avon in 2020, Natura committed to help Avon achieve B-Corp certification by 2026.[6]

As part of the assessment for B-Corp status, companies have to commit in their articles of association to take social and environmental considerations into account alongside commercial in their decision-making. B-Corp is an accreditation rather than legal status, but it does illustrate the move towards new models and sits alongside the growing questioning of the social legitimacy – if not the legality – of the tax arrangements of many multinational businesses and the transfer of revenue to low-tax jurisdictions. In the UK, for example, the Better Business Act movement is aiming to change the law to make sure every company has to align the interests of their shareholders with those of wider society and the environment.

Increased transparency leads inevitably towards greater questioning of the social legitimacy of all business practices, and of course accusations of hypocrisy for those businesses that profess a social purpose on the one hand, yet turn out to be short-changing society with the other.

And in all this we hear the question of whether the 2008 financial crisis marked the end of the neoliberal consensus and the suggestion that the closer integration of business with society and planet, as posited in the Sustainable Development Goals, might replace it.

The rising power of a Generation Z willing and able to "cancel" companies who don't live up to their expectations; the increasing focus by investors on ESG criteria in assessing the strength of businesses; the dawning reality of climate change and the response to it in legislation from California to China. All are shifting tectonic plates with a set direction and their impact on business has been accelerated by the pandemic. And all businesses will have to ask themselves how they need to go about building a sustainable brand in this new normal.

•••

Lifebuoy soap has come a long way since that visit to Kibera in 2006. It has now helped over a billion people develop better handwashing habits[7]; its partnerships extend from UN organisations to national governments to NGOs across the world; in the five years from 2008 it grew from a €250 to a €600 million brand; and in 2020 it came home to the UK, and full circle from Kibera to West Kirby, on a mission to help its country of birth respond to its biggest emergency in a generation.[8]

Lifebuoy's story is one of a brand that discovered – or rather rediscovered – its social mission and delivered commercial success by putting that mission at the heart of its business strategy. That approach has taken Lifebuoy from its South Asia stronghold through the rest of Asia and into shops and homes across Africa and Latin America and now back home to the UK. Its quest to help a billion people protect themselves from disease through the simple act of hand washing with soap has driven that business growth. It is fostering innovation in public health behaviour change, winning government and funder support for handwashing programmes in schools, attracting consumers with its values and inspiring communications. It has been a mainstay in the progress of the Unilever Sustainable Living Plan and all that is achieving for one of the world's most wide-reaching multinationals, a company whose brands touch two billion people every day.

The connection between its social and commercial objectives – encouraging more handwashing with soap prevents disease and increases sales – is in one sense very simple, but the examples are multiplying of other brands and corporations who are following the same principles. Brands like Andrex and Domestos are tackling sanitation; Nike and Always promoting equality; retailers like Sainsbury's and Marks & Spencer, Walmart and Carrefour see where their shoppers are headed and want to demonstrate not only that they share those values but that they can help show them the way. Corporations like GlaxoSmithKline and ManpowerGroup are focussing their support on areas most closely aligned to their businesses. Multinationals like Coca-Cola and Nestlé state that their future prosperity depends on refinding their social missions and demonstrating how they can make a positive contribution to society.

The transparency and interconnectedness of the digital age are changing everything. In this context it is not surprising that the Millennials who have grown up in this age, and Generation Z who have known nothing else, are alive to all the implications of doing business and demand that the companies they buy from and work for not only take account of these societal and environmental externalities but also aspire to a higher purpose. Nor is it surprising that they are more comfortable with those companies saying they can make a profit out of having a social mission, given that they themselves say they want to work for purpose-driven organisations and earn a decent salary.

Lifebuoy, a simple bar of soap, a brand over 130 years old, has shown – in an age of technological advances unimaginable when William Lever launched his brand by the banks of the Mersey – that the old idea of a business being a part of society, rather than apart from it, is relevant today. In fact, it is more relevant when those technological advances have opened businesses up to unprecedented scrutiny and challenge. The Lifebuoys of 130 years' time will be those sustainable brands that have understood and embraced the opportunities offered by forming a closer relationship with society.

NOTES

1 https://www.ikea.com/gb/en/this-is-ikea/about-us/vision-and-business-idea-pub9cd02291.

2 https://www.mondaq.com/india/corporate-governance/366528/corporate-social-responsibility--indian-companies-act-2013.

3 Indu Goel and Nick Wingfield (1 December 2015). Mark Zuckerberg vows to donate 99% of his Facebook shares for charity. http://www.nytimes.com/2015/12/02/technology/mark-zuckerberg-facebook-charity.html?_r=0.

4 https://www.thejournal.ie/brazil-water-shortage-1946758-Feb2015/.

5 https://bcorporation.net/about-b-corps.

6 https://bcorporation.net/zbtcz03z23/bcm/b-corps-doing-business-better-screening-supply-chains-positive-impact.

7 https://www.unilever.com/planet-and-society/health-and-wellbeing/handwashing-for-life/.

8 https://www.thegrocer.co.uk/buying-and-supplying/unilever-to-bring-lifebuoy-hygiene-brand-back-to-uk/646949.article.

INDEX